Single.
On
Purpose.

HarperOne
An Imprint of HarperCollins*Publishers*

REDEFINE EVERYTHING

Single.
On
Purpose.

FIND YOURSELF FIRST

JOHN KIM

HarperCollins books may be purchased for educational, business, or sales promotional use. For information, please email the Special Markets Department at SPsales@harpercollins.com.

FIRST EDITION

Designed by Janet Evans-Scanlon

Library of Congress Cataloging-in-Publication Data is available upon request.

ISBN 978-0-06-298073-1
ISBN 978-0-06-307371-5 (Intl)

21 22 23 24 25 LSC 10 9 8 7 6 5 4 3 2 1

DISCLAIMER

This is *not* an anti-relationship book. This is a pro-relationship (with yourself) book.

CONTENTS

ACT III

The New You

Sometimes you have to stand alone to prove to others and yourself that you can still stand.

—UNKNOWN

Single.
On
Purpose.

Introduction

've been single. Many times. I've struggled with loneliness. Rejection. Not believing I was desirable. I've tried "dating myself" again and again, and it was bullshit. The truth is, we're humans and we're not meant to do life alone. We want to love someone. And that's okay. We're biologically built that way. What's not okay is losing ourselves because we don't have someone to love. Or losing ourselves in the person we've chosen to love.

I have struggled with singlehood and also lost myself in relationships. I have jumped into things way too fast after a breakup was still fresh. Within days, I've been "back on the market," swiping to find someone else to lose myself in. Because I didn't want to be alone. Because I didn't want to eat by myself. Because I like sex too much. But on a deeper level, because I needed to prove to myself that I was desirable, lovable, and worthy. And it's really hard to feel that on a Friday night when you're at home eating your feelings.

Out of desperation, I've contacted exes and later regretted it. I have wondered how many "ones" have gotten away. I have felt that deep loneliness, the kind that keeps you from washing your hair or wearing anything but sweats. I have done all the things: Gotten together with women I wasn't that into. Been rejected by women I was really into. Tried to be someone I wasn't for someone else. Forced things that didn't feel right because I wanted it to work. And of course, eaten way too much ice cream in one sitting.

Deep inside, I knew I needed to be single. On purpose. I've been in relationships constantly since I was twenty-two, and I knew I needed to build a better one with myself before I could build anything healthy and meaningful with anyone else. I knew I needed to process my own shit. Break patterns. Find a sense of self. Not be codependent. And work on areas of my life other than love. **Because there's more to life than who we choose to love.** It may not feel like that right now. But trust me, there is.

I learned this after a divorce, when I was finally forced to look at myself, *by* myself, without the buffer of another person. The divorce forced me to reevaluate my entire life. Really examine what I was doing and why. Although painful, it was the best thing that's ever happened to me. Because it was the first domino of my singlehood journey to connect me back to myself. For the first time in my life I *chose* to be alone.

In the beginning, it sucked balls. It was miserable. Who would I kiss? Hold? Stay in and make love to and watch documentaries with when it was rainy outside? Who the fuck was going to scratch my back? And what about the weekend? What was I going to do by myself? Who was I going to do nothing with? Because doing nothing alone isn't the same as doing nothing with someone else. Doing nothing with someone else means you've really found love. Doing nothing by yourself means you're a loser. Fuck, it was going to be so easy deciding where to eat now. It felt like my life was over.

These were the thoughts sprinting through my mind as panic set in. But I had to tell myself I was choosing it. It was a decision that I don't usually make, and I had to believe I would come out the other side better because of it. That's what breaking a pattern looks like. Not just for me, but for all the clients I would go on to help. That was the fuel for me, the 92 octane. So I did it. And I am not going to lie. It was hard. Like, addiction recovery hard. But I took it a day at a time, like they say in the meetings. And slowly but surely, it got easier. Not only did it get easier, I became different. Things started shifting on the inside. I started to grow.

As I started doing the inner work (which I'll get into later), I was able to do the outer work. Or more accurately, I wasn't able to *not* do it. Because when inner change happens, it naturally ripples outward. It's like when you realize you can't eat the entire bag of chips in one sitting like you used to when you were in your twenties. Something has permanently changed inside, like this new behavior of putting the chips away before the bag is empty, maybe even using a chip clip. There was a lot of this happening for me at the time. So I decided to write about it. I started a blog called *The Angry Therapist* and wrote with vulnerability for the first time in my life. No more clever dialogue hoping to sell the million-dollar screenplay. I just wrote my truth. Soon I had followers, then emails and Skype sessions and a full practice of clients who wanted no-bullshit advice from someone they could relate to. Ironically, my greatest relationship failure was the catalyst for giving relationship advice—the main reason people wanted guidance from me.

The motivation to write this book came from coaching thousands of people in the last decade who experienced severe depression because they were single. Many of them had successful careers. Many of them had amazing friends. But because they had no one to kiss in the morning and do nothing with on a Friday night, they saw themselves as failures. They internalized the idea of not having a partner as being defective. Most had been in nothing but shitty, toxic, lopsided relationships, and yet being single was worse. They figured something was wrong with them, and they came to me to find out what that was. A lot of them were in their thirties or forties, and they felt like time was running out. They felt the sand in the hourglass draining as they lost more and more hope.

A Typical Session

COFFEE SHOP—EARLY MORNING

John is buried in his laptop when he notices a woman in her early thirties standing in front of him.

JOHN
Hey.

CHRISTY
Hi.

CHRISTY (*before she even takes a seat*)

I told my boyfriend I've been thinking about someone else, and he broke up with me.

JOHN

Oh, I'm sorry. (*closes his laptop and gets situated for his session*)

CHRISTY

I have a friend named Dion. We're working on a project together. There's crazy sexual chemistry. Before you ask, no, he's not good for me. I know this. But I can't stop thinking about him.

JOHN

You told your boyfriend this?

CHRISTY

Technically my ex as of yesterday. I realized on a retreat at Joshua Tree. Yes, I was on mushrooms, but I had this revelation. I was only with him because it made sense. I've never really been attracted to him, and it's not fair to him.

JOHN

Okay, let's put a bookmark there. Tell me about some of your other previous relationships. Would you like a coffee?

CHRISTY

No, I'm good. I lost my virginity when I was fourteen. I don't really remember it, though. (*A few patrons glance over. John's used to this. He does sessions here all the time. His client doesn't notice or mind.*)

CHRISTY

I was in a nine-year relationship with someone verbally

abusive. Then another one that was a nightmare, well, not in the beginning, but you know . . .

JOHN
Have you been in anything healthy?

CHRISTY
No, except for this last one that I just ruined.

JOHN
So your current relationship is over. It was healthy, but you were not sexually attracted to him. And the person you are sexually attracted to is toxic and bad for you. And you know this.

CHRISTY
Right. Which one should I go with?

JOHN
Yourself.

CHRISTY
Huh?

JOHN
Why are those the only choices?

CHRISTY
Because they're the only ones in my life right now.

JOHN
I think you need to be single. (*beat*) On purpose.

(*Christy looks flabbergasted.*)

I've had hundreds of sessions just like this. Different stories, but all the same. It's why I wrote this book. We don't know how to be single. It's a journey most do not embark on.

It's time to reframe the narrative of being single and embrace what I learned when I finally chose to be alone:

The Richest Soil for Growth Is Cultivated When You're Single

When you're in a relationship, you're less motivated to examine the black box of what happened in your previous relationships. You're in something new now. You've ran away from the crash. You've moved on. That door has closed. So the chances of you fully processing and taking ownership of your part in the expiration, of learning and growing and becoming a better version of yourself, are exponentially low. Especially if you've jumped into a new relationship shortly after the old one, which most of us do.

That is why the growth soil is so rich during the times between relationships. You have a limited amount of time to work on yourself and your life before you meet someone else. It doesn't mean you can't grow when you're in a relationship. (This book is about that too—more on that later.) But let's face it. When you're in a relationship, you're building something with someone else. You're a part of something else. So it's imperative to take advantage of the time you're unattached. Instead of searching for someone to be with, you must explore you. Your patterns. Your definitions. How you love and why. Your dreams. The dent you want to make in this world. You must explore your relationship with self. **You must be with yourself first.**

My goal in writing this book is to start that process for you. To introduce you to you—for many of you, maybe for the first time.

First, we must get rid of one of the greatest misconceptions about life, the idea that you can't be happy unless you are with someone. I've coached thousands of singles over the years, and every single one of them believed when they came to me that they couldn't be happy unless they found a partner. Unless they were married. Unless they had someone to come home to. Their singlehood meant they were incomplete or defective. Less than. They believed there was something wrong with them.

The truth is, you don't have to be in a relationship to be happy. Sure, a relationship can bring you lots of joy. There's nothing wrong with wanting to be in a relationship—we're all human. But a relationship is not *required* for you to be happy. It's not the only way to find joy in your life. Your happiness isn't contingent on loving someone else. That's something that's been programmed into you by movies, advertising, social norms, social media, and old blueprints.

The world has been waving this flag in your face since you were given your first Barbie doll and then quickly added a Ken doll to complete the picture. But Barbie never needed Ken. All she needed was that convertible Vette. It was the world telling her she needed a house and a man. (And we never even gave Ken a job or a personality. Or asked him if he liked women.)

It's finally time to empower singlehood and provide better blueprints for building happiness. It's time to shatter old definitions and smash that loud internal ticking clock. It's time to scrape away the *shoulds*. Rip down the Norman Rockwell painting, kick a hole in it, and finally give "single" the fucking superhero cape it deserves.

This Book Is For . . .

Anyone who believes they are less than or defective because they haven't found "the one" or "true love." Anyone who is sick and tired of swiping, being catfished, being ghosted on. Those who are done with the dick pics, double standards, and one-night stands. Anyone wondering if they can still have kids. Anyone who feels hopeless, lonely, or frustrated and doesn't know what to do about it.

This book is also for anyone who is currently in a relationship but the dynamic has changed. You've drifted. Grown apart. The "in love" has turned to "in lost," and neither of you know yourself anymore. There's lots of finger-pointing, sex is scheduled or doesn't happen at all, and you've both lost touch with the individuals you were when you came together. You might have complaints about your partner but are coming to realize that it's not really about them. It's not about changing anyone or "fixing" the relationship. You have no more energy for that. It's about starting with you.

Because here's the thing: **Singlehood isn't just about being single. Singlehood is about being a whole person.** Even when you're in a relationship. In fact, especially when you're in a relationship. Singlehood is about not defining yourself by or being dependent on your relationship. It's about having a healthy relationship with yourself first. But many of us lose ourselves in relationships. We become a smaller part of a whole, consumed by something greater—the relationship with our partner. Or we enter relationships in pieces, hoping the relationship or our partner will put us back together. And we all know how that ends.

A thriving relationship is one in which two whole people come together and do life *with* each other, not *at* or *around* each other. To do that, we must have a healthy relationship with ourselves, but who teaches us how to do that? There's no general education requirement in school that covers boundaries, independence, and knowledge of self. And healthy relationships with themselves sure as hell don't come naturally to most people. Humans don't come with an owner's manual, so we never learn how to truly take care of, connect to, and build a healthy relationship with ourselves. We know what conditioner works the best on our hair. We know what foods we need to stay away from. We know how to take care of other people. But we don't know how to feed our soul. We don't know how to draw boundaries with Sharpie instead of chalk. We don't know how to recharge. We don't know how to dissolve our cognitive distortions. We don't know how to unshackle who we *are* from what we *do*. We don't know how to truly love ourselves. Not in a "checking off a list" way from reading self-help books, but in a deeply honest and sustainable way that changes us from the inside out. A way that makes us understand and accept our story. That makes us know who we are and what our value is.

And finally, this book is for anyone who has never been

single. Ever. You've always been in a relationship, maybe since high school, jumping from one lily pad to another and repeating the same dysfunctional patterns over and over. The only thing changing is the faces. Your friends all say, "You need to be alone," and you reply, "I don't know how!" They think you're full of shit, but the truth is, you're afraid. You're uncomfortable with yourself. It's so much easier to hide in someone else. But hiding in a relationship or another person shrinks your ability to expand and explore your potential as a human being. You know this. And you know you need to work on building your relationship with yourself. But you don't know how. You need a road map.

From Angry to Author

When I first started my blog *The Angry Therapist*, I didn't think anyone would read it. To be honest, I was super-alone and just needed a way to pass the time. I needed a distraction from myself and my loneliness. I was in a bad place, and I didn't want to face it head on. So I thought funneling my energy into a blank screen every day would help. But what actually happened was the beginning of reconnecting with myself. As I documented my journey and life transition on the blog, I started having revelations. For the first time in my life, I felt something. Not just about me and what I was going through at the time, but about the possibility that my story could help others. And how resources like a blog or the internet could be used as therapeutic tools. *The Angry Therapist* gave me not only a voice but also, for the first time in my life, a sense of purpose. I didn't know this at the time, but I wasn't angry just because I was hurting. I was angry because I had realized that the clinical system, how we help people and how we become helpers, was broken.

I found my true north and ran there as fast as I could. I started coaching people around the world, using webcams, meeting them in coffee shops, and taking them on hikes. I started a life coach training intensive in my kitchen in my underwear and taught all the classes without knowing what the hell I was doing. All I knew was that there needed to be a new way to help people help others that didn't require eating Top Ramen for six years to avoid defaulting on student loans, then burning out and working with a board breathing down your neck. That realization led to developing the intensive therapeutic approach called JRNI coaching, which now has over one thousand trained practitioners. The energy from this initiative led to my first book deal. Then another one. And now *Single*, my third book. All this is to say that if you muster the courage to start working on yourself instead of just focusing on who you're going to love, the universe will work through you to make your story bigger than you. Then, when you meet someone who deserves you, you will only bring more to the table as a whole person who is going somewhere. Or, if you're currently in a relationship, you will have found more meaning and a sense of worth in yourself and won't demand that from your partner. Your relationship will be more balanced, healthy, and sustainable.

Like everything I write, this book will be coming *with* you, not *at* you. I try to bring things down to street level. Because self-help doesn't have to be complicated. And it's better when it's coming from a real, lived experience—including painful mistakes. That's what I'm trying to bring you in this book—the stories of my clients, what I've learned from them, and most of all, my own adventure connecting back to myself. Think of this book as my *Eat, Pray, Love*. But instead of traveling to exotic locations around the world, eating amazing foods, having passionate love affairs, and praying to God in ancient temples, I got tattoos, rediscovered Los Angeles on my motorcycle, and ate a lot of doughnuts. I worked out. Cried. Blogged. I went on my inner journey and came back to the village changed. The truth is, most people can't change their day-to-day and go travel the world when they're going through their rebirth. They still have to hit an alarm clock, go to work, and take care of people. But that doesn't mean they can't rebuild themselves. They can still grow, evolve, and change. That's how I did it.

I'm not just a therapist who has helped thousands rewrite their stories. I'm also a hopeless romantic who sought approval and validation and tried to fill a void in myself by being with women. I was broke and had nothing but a blog and a webcam. I was someone who struggled with codependency and unhealthy attachment. Who was exposed to sexual images at an early age and struggled (still do) with true intimacy. Who used love as a drug. Who always lived in his head, disconnected from his body, and had no sense of purpose or sense of self. My point is, I have a complicated story, just like you do. I've been through some shit, just like you have. And I didn't come out the other side. Because there is no other side. Your journey never ends. It just changes as you change. But the journey only happens if you decide to go on it. There is a call to action. If you decide not to embark on the voyage, you will always live in the past. You will stay muted. Angry. Miserable. Incomplete.

If you do decide to accept your call (everything that has happened to get you here right now as you're reading this), your relationship with yourself will strengthen and you will take ownership of your life. You will evolve and start living closer to your truth and potential. Your whole outlook will change, and great things will happen. Things you would not have seen with your old outlook.

You're not going to find someone by reading this book. But I promise that you'll be a better person if and when you do. Because this book isn't about finding someone else. It's about finding you.

ACT I

The Self

(Connecting Back to You)

There are more single adults living, working, and yes, still breathing, in the United States than ever before in history. In 2017, the US census reported 110.6 million unmarried people over the age of 18—that's 45.2 percent of the American adult population—carrying out their lives to a new set of societal norms. Are unmarried Americans doomed, or on to something truly exciting?

—BELLA DEPAULO, social scientist and author of *Singled Out: How Singles Are Stereotyped, Stigmatized, and Ignored, and Still Live Happily Ever After*

How to Deal
with Loneliness

Loneliness is a real thing when you're single. That's why I'm starting there—because most of us experience it. I get it. I've been there. Many times. Forget the empowering anthem "I don't need anyone else but myself right now." Although that is true, it requires a journey to get there. Saying the words without taking that journey doesn't bring you automatic empowerment—just an empty pledge to a fake flag.

I'll tell you why you feel lonely. Because what you get from an intimate partner is something you can't get from anyone else. Because those conversations after work and those waffles on Saturday morning help the world make sense. Because spooning puts you to sleep like a little baby. Because tongues feel fucking good. Because looking into someone's eyes for longer than three seconds reminds you that we're not meant to do life alone. Because being emotionally naked makes you feel alive. Because you can't really tell your friends how your day went every single day or you won't have any friends. Because we're meant to give and share, lose ourselves and find ourselves through others, and love, hard. Because ordering in is so much better when you have someone.

You feel lonely because you want these things and you haven't found someone to experience them with. And that's okay. There's no reason to skirt that and force yourself to go on some kind of *Eat, Pray, Love* journey to autocorrect your emotional self. Unless you feel like that is what you need. But for many—and by many I mean most—we're just lonely because we haven't found someone to love. That's it. Stop judging and labeling it. If you haven't slept, you're going to feel tired. If you haven't loved anyone in a while, you're going to crave that experience and feel lonely.

But there's a difference between the feeling of loneliness and "I am lonely." One is an experience, a feeling that comes and goes. The other is an identity, tightly tied to your sense of worth. Instead of just being aware of the feeling, you have attached added meaning to it. You *are* lonely. Because you feel lonely, you believe there is something wrong with you. You're too old or too fat or whatever. But it's not your fault. That knot has been tied by society. Whether you know it or not, you have been programmed. Think about it: How many shows or movies have you seen where the protagonist *doesn't* find love and is still happy? How many *don't* get the girl? Or *never* find their man? Loneliness is the struggle that needs to be overcome. Once you conquer it, only then will you feel happy.

You can understand the roots of this feeling, but understanding it doesn't take away how real and constant it is. It's not temporary, like being hungry or horny. It's an ongoing state that can make you lose hope and wonder, *Will I ever find love again?* I'm not going to try to prove you wrong with logic. You feel what you feel and that shit is real. I know. I've felt it. When we feel loneliness for long enough, we start to believe no one wants to be with us. We start to believe we will always be alone. I know I did. The loneliness grows into hopelessness. It's a one-two punch.

But you are not lonely the way that you have brown eyes or small feet. It's time to reevaluate the situation. You need to redefine your old concepts and stop assuming that being *alone* is the same as being *lonely*.

First, stop ruminating while you're having that lonesome feeling. Stop feeding it. Stop asking yourself if you will ever find the kind of person you've always dreamed of. Maybe you won't. But if that shakes your world, the *last* thing you need to be in right now is a relationship. Because that desperation will only poison whatever relationship you do find yourself in. So let's address your fear right now, head on. Take a deep breath and ask yourself the following question, preferably a few times: **What if you never find a partner?**

Did your heart stop? It might have for a second, but despite what you may feel, you're still very much alive. Listen, I'm not saying you will never find love. I'm saying that this looming question you allow to follow you around like a dark cloud is what's stripping the vibrance out of your life. This giant *what-if* you keep asking yourself is preventing you from truly living. Instead, you are waiting around for something to happen to you, and that waiting produces the feeling of loneliness. But it's actually not loneliness you're struggling with. At the core, it's the deep belief that you will *always* be alone. It's hopelessness. That's what's crippling. To turn the lights on and get rid of this heavy shadow, you must face this belief head on. How? Accept it. Fully.

> **Radical acceptance is the practice of accepting life on life's terms and not resisting what you cannot change. Radical acceptance is about saying yes to life, just as it is.**

In this case, singlehood. This doesn't mean giving up on love. This doesn't mean denying your wants. And it certainly doesn't mean taking yourself "off the market," deleting all your dating apps, and staying home every night. It actually means the complete opposite: Go out and live. Stop waiting, hoping, and being afraid.

Before you can do this, though, you must be okay with the possibility of never finding your one. Again, that doesn't mean you won't. Acceptance just means that, if you don't find the one, your world will not end. The sky will not fall. You will still build a wonderful and meaningful life. I've helped many clients build amazing lives without a partner. Clients who came to see me because they felt incomplete and less than because they hadn't found their one. People who started to move their life chips from *we* to *me* and started to bet on themselves. They built things, like a business, a better body, meaningful friendships. And eventually they built a happier life. They ate at new restaurants. They started painting again. They took dance classes. Got passionate about fitness. Learned to ride motorcycles. Or to speak a second language. They climbed rocks. Traveled and quit jobs they dreaded showing up for. They fed new passions and did whatever they wanted. They found freedom and comfort in their own self and realized that, yes, you can want a partner, but life doesn't have to stop because you don't have one.

The more you accept this truth, the sooner you will stop feeling that being single is linked to a lower sense of worth, the less you will tell yourself you need to find someone to be happy, and the more you will be present in your life instead of obsessing about the future. Accepting this truth, you will start to run toward yourself instead of into the arms of the next person to come along. And when you do meet someone—because of course you will—you will bring a more interesting, alluring set of skills and experiences to the table. Instead of meeting someone who will save you from your situation, you will meet someone who can share your current joys.

Look, no one wants to be alone. Not you. Not me. We all want to share our life with someone else. Ten years ago, the question *What if I never find a partner?* would have sunk my soul. Imagining myself doing life alone terrified me. No one to share meals with. No one to hold or think about. Who would I sext? Go on staycations with? But ten years ago, I didn't have much of a life. And that's the difference between me then and me now. I'm not any less of a hopeless romantic. I don't want love any less. I just have a richer and more complete life now. A life that doesn't hang on being with someone. *This* is what gave me my power back. Asking myself *Where am I going?* before asking myself *Who is going with me?*

Love and relationships are only one part of your life, not your entire life. There are so many other aspects of your life that are meaningful and fulfilling. Your art. Your career. Exercising your voice and the dent you're going to make in this world. Your friendships. Your family. Your passions and hobbies. Your curiosity leading you to explore, learn, grow, and expand. When you actually build your own life, a life that is honest to you and stands on its own, the fear of being alone starts to fade.

I Found Myself through Doughnuts, Barbells, and a Motorcycle

Here's what happens. As kids, we weren't just curious and fearless, climbing trees barefoot and seeking adventure. Most of us also went through a shitstorm. We got bullied and made fun of for wearing the same shirt or for not having a tradable lunch. We saw our parents throw chairs, get divorced, or drink too much. Money was a thing—there was never enough. So we had to grow up fast, get jobs, take care of our siblings. If you're a woman, you were taught to be nice, helpful, and quiet. Your boundaries were crossed. Something was taken from you. If not your virginity, your voice. Three out of five women I help experienced some kind of sexual abuse or assault while growing up. That's the truth, and if you don't start with truth, you're really not starting. If you're a man, you were taught—if not by your dad, then by locker rooms and society—to pull yourself up by your bootstraps, suppress your feelings, and "man up."

All of this wires us a certain way. We become afraid, emotionally stunted, and vulnerable. We attach ourselves to others, and to their opinions of us, because we don't have a strong sense of self. But our souls haven't been crushed by shitty jobs and lopsided relationships yet. We don't know anything about credit card debt, or taxes, or rejection. We haven't been cheated on, lied to, or ghosted. Fear and false beliefs have not hijacked us yet. Our mental dial is locked on "Explore." We want to jump off things. To learn what ants taste like. There's so much to do. Every day is an adventure, the world is big, and in that world we are curious and fearless.

As we move into adulthood, we discover we are different. We're not as pretty, tall, athletic, or smart as others. So we do everything we can to fit in. Some of us make it into the circle. Some of us don't. The ones who don't become outcasts. We start to believe we are less than, so we try to make up for it in other ways. This starts the disconnect with ourselves. Our search for what we're lacking sets off the toxic pattern of living from the outside in instead of from the inside out. We lock away parts of ourselves that we once liked in a hope chest. We become lesser versions of ourselves so others will like us. Or we posture. Either way, we hide now and learn to chase approval and validation, a quest we will stay on for many years to come. Soon it turns us invisible.

Then, we get into relationships. We feel a sense of worth and importance. We feel desirable. And because we finally feel seen, we believe we have found ourselves. But what actually has happened is that we have begun losing ourselves in someone else. We discover codependency, unhealthy love, and heartbreak. Over and over. Eventually, we believe we are not only defective but unlovable. We develop poor coping strategies that create a pattern of self-destruction. This creates more disconnection as we lose trust in others, but more importantly in ourselves. We become putty, moldable by others. We do anything we can do to prove we actually matter, have value, and are lovable. We buy things to fill a void and lock our dial on "Achieve."

Life continues to chip away at us as we search for purpose and meaning but come up short. The frustration strips us of our curiosity. All we seem to have found is judgment, and the magic of the world fades. We have seen how the movie is made. We punch clocks instead of the sky and chase blueprints that don't even belong to us, usually those of our parents and society. We make sacrifices because we believe that's what being an adult looks like. We put our own needs and wants aside for others. We continue to lose ourselves in relationships (disconnect) instead of building a healthy relationship with ourselves (connect) and remain completely unaware of what a healthy relationship even looks like. After all, we've never experienced one. So we get into toxic, abusive, and lopsided relationships because they feel familiar, though they bring us the kind of pain that makes us question life. We keep that buried deep inside and pretend it's all good.

We continue to push through, to chase things that are not honest to us, falling into the same patterns that create the same experiences and cement the same beliefs. Life becomes a giant crowbar that pries us apart, splitting us in half. I know, a bit dramatic, but we are not aware that this is happening. Because it's happening on the inside. On the outside, life is life and we have accepted it. What exactly is happy anyway? Come on. Is anyone really happy? So we keep going. Putting in long hours. Compromising. Taking care of others. Swiping. Negotiating in relationships. Not telling people what we really think. We move forward instead of inward and start fading like Michael J. Fox in *Back to the Future* when he couldn't get his parents back together. Our internal scales go out of balance, and the world begins to shrink. What was once an ocean is now a plastic swimming pool. With cracks in it. We have created our own prison. Same shit, different day.

Years blur into a decade, and we drift so far we have no idea who we are or what we want anymore. Happy is disappearing in the rearview as we watch the road ahead with aging eyes, and fast-food wrappers on our laps. We have accepted our circumstances. This is as good as it's going to get. So we numb with food, drugs, meaningless sex.

We continue to drift further from ourselves, and the more we disconnect from ourselves, the more we crave connecting with someone else.

Read that sentence again. This is why so many of us fall into lukewarm relationships that lead to years of misery and heartbreak. Relationships we know aren't right but we don't want to be alone. Or we think we can fix because fixing things is how we find value in ourselves. But we can't fix other people. And we'll always only be 50 percent of any relationship. So even if we could be perfect, that would be only half and half is not enough.

It's easier to get into a relationship to "fix" a feeling of hopelessness or boredom. But the call is coming from inside the house—until you resolve it, the disconnect with who you really are is going to haunt you. No perfect partner can replace that. You have to deal with it at some point.

My Bathroom Stall Moment

felt like I was sinking with cinder blocks strapped to my ankles, like in Mafia movies. My marriage was falling apart. I had changed careers from screenwriter to therapist and was questioning whether I had made the right decision. Partly because I was in a job that was shady as fuck. I had just graduated from therapy school and was working as a counselor at a Russian "treatment" center, i.e., a clubhouse for the elderly. Basically a place where people made insurance money off elderly non-English-speaking Russians. So what was I doing there if I didn't know a lick of Russian? I was signing off on paperwork and writing case notes. They weren't fake, but were they real? Was I really doing therapy or was I babysitting the dying? It got so bad that I would lock myself in a bathroom stall and wait until someone found me. It was a game I'd play, seeing if I could stay in the stall longer each time. But I couldn't quit this job. It was my way out. Tucking in a button-down shirt every day and earning a paycheck was going to save my marriage. Even if it sucked out my soul.

I've never felt so alone in my life. I remember the day when, hiding in the bathroom stall as usual, I was resting my head against the wall and blankly staring into space and suddenly the dam broke. Tears flooded down like a river, but with no expression or sound. I just sat there, blankly staring. The tears were the only proof that I was alive. Well, that and my name coming over the PA: *John Kim, you are needed.* I imagined the voice was coming from God. So I said something back: *If I get up, please help me.* It was a short prayer. I hadn't talked to God in a very long time. But the prayer fell on deaf ears. God didn't respond.

I had told myself I wasn't going to let myself fall into another shitty job. I once worked graveyard shifts wearing a hazmat suit and peeling plasma for minimum wage. But I was fifteen then, and actually liked who I was. My friends and I purposely found the worst job we could just so we could say we did it. We were "rebellious." We were teenagers, and the men we worked with were in their thirties and forties. I remembered how ghostly they looked. Like walking shells, zombies. I remembered feeling sorry for them and vowing never to be like them when I grew up. And yet here I was, in my thirties, and just like them. Instead of a Coleman lunchbox, I carried a *Diagnostic and Statistical Manual 5.* I didn't know who I was. At all. I was completely disconnected from myself. A few weeks later, my wife asked for a separation, which shortly turned into a divorce. And that snapped me.

Or at least I thought it did. But things don't just break people out of nowhere. What breaks us is not losing a job, or friends, or even a marriage. What breaks us is drifting away from ourselves for too long. It's not a single event. It's that gradual drift. For years I was writing screenplays in coffee shops. That's all I did. I didn't have a life. I didn't have any friends. I didn't have any hobbies. I just woke up, dragged myself to a coffee shop, and punched keys all fucking day until the sun went down. Day in, day out. And by the way, I was doing it for the wrong reason. If screenwriting and I were in a relationship, I had checked out a long time ago. I didn't love writing movies anymore. I was chasing the wrong thing. I thought it would make me rich, i.e., happy.

Doing things for the outcome rather than for the joy of the process disconnects you from yourself. You start chasing. You get desperate. You forget your "why." But most importantly, you don't allow yourself to be happy until you get what you want. And if that never comes, you never practice being happy. (Yes, happy is built through daily practice. It's not a light switch to flip on or a destination to arrive at.) So instead of practicing happy, I just worried and dreaded and saw the glass as half empty. The sky was always falling. This mindset kept me trapped, stunted, and in a low-grade fight-or-flight state. You can't enjoy life when your body thinks it's dying. It made me hollow.

We are not born just to do things. Or just to love other people. Our potency and our path forward are first found in our connection with ourselves. And it's through this connection, this evolving, growing, expanding relationship with ourselves, that we honestly, genuinely, and meaningfully do things and love people.

How I Connected Back to Me

I never felt so alone and I've never felt so alive.

—THIRD EYE BLIND

had no idea or plan. Yes, I was studying psychology and on my way to becoming a therapist. But that didn't mean shit. Just because I wanted to help others didn't mean I had helped myself. Maybe helping others was a way to not look at my own shit. I don't know, but I was clueless. I hadn't done any real work. A handful of individual therapy sessions and some couples counseling isn't real work. A master's degree isn't real work. Reading psychology books isn't real work. Blogging self-betterment listicles isn't real work. Real work comes from going through the journey, not just from absorbing information. That's the problem with self-betterment today. I don't give a fuck if you know Reiki. What have you been through and how has that changed you? I had no idea I was about to embark on a journey, from crying in a bathroom stall to reuniting with a sense of self I hadn't felt since I was a kid. It turns out that God did talk to me. Just not through words. God talked to me through the events and people who appeared in my life.

Barbells and Doughnuts (My Body)

After my divorce, I was introduced to an Asian guy by someone at church. His name was Sam, and he was also a therapist in his thirties going through a divorce. Sam had also left a career in entertainment—broadcast news. He also was a beta male who used to ask his wife if he could buy sugared cereal. We had a lot in common. Anyway, we hit it off right away and moved in together in a run-down condo in Koreatown owned by his friend (a cheap rent hookup) known as "Heartbreak Hotel"—everyone who lived there was dealing with a broken heart.

Sam was my first real Asian friend. I grew up in a predominantly white neighborhood in the 1980s. We weren't Asians then. We were Orientals. Like rugs. We weren't cool. And if you weren't cool, you got your ass kicked. So I tried to be as "white" as possible. They used to call me a Twinkie. Yellow on the outside, white on the inside. Sam grew up in an all-Black neighborhood. I guess he was more of a banana iced chocolate cupcake? The point is, we both knew what it felt like to be at odds with who we were and where we came from.

In a strange way, Sam connected me back to myself. To my roots, if you will. We got each other. I wish I could say we were like Starsky and Hutch, but to be honest, we were more like the male Asian version of Laverne and Shirley. He was definitely Laverne. We both had a sweet tooth and ate a lot of doughnuts. I think it was a way of making up for all the times we couldn't when we were married. One of our nightly routines was to drive to a Yogurtland in Hollywood. (We knew that people who ate ice cream hated themselves, so we ate frozen yogurt.) Right next to the Yogurtland was what looked like an adult playground. No, not a porn shop. It was a gym but with monkey bars, giant tires, and gymnastic rings. It was called CrossFit, and it was a brand-new way of doing fitness.

When I was a kid, I used to break-dance. I used to completely lose myself in it, spending hours spinning on my head after school, hitting flow states and losing track of time. It was my favorite thing to do. When I break-danced, I was fully connected to my body. There was no separation. My body and I were one, and break-dancing made me feel complete. Then I had to grow up. Put away my parachute pants and fat laces. And of course, I slowly disconnected from my body.

Since then, I had always gone to the gym but only for aesthetic purposes, just to look better. I had no feelings associated with working out. I lifted a lot of weights only so I could fill out my T-shirts. I never did legs. I didn't know what a squat was. I looked like a pigeon. Sam and I wanted abs. We were single and on the prowl. But that's not why I got obsessed with CrossFit. After my first workout there, something felt different. CrossFit connected me to that eleven-year-old again. In practicing muscle-ups, pull-ups, and handstand push-ups, I pulled out that kid I had locked away for so long and restarted my relationship with him. I got to taste adrenaline and dopamine through movement again, and it made me feel alive.

Sam and I CrossFitted every day. It became a part of our

routine. Once or three times a week, we would treat ourselves with doughnuts afterwards. But this time, we weren't eating our feelings. We had earned that shit. We were allowing ourselves something we wanted, something we deserved. We were connecting with a part of ourselves that we had stuffed away years ago when we were married. Through barbells and doughnuts, I started to connect back to me.

Now, think back to your own version of break-dancing freedom. When did you feel the most comfortable in your body? What's changed since then? What happened that disconnected you from your body? Marriage? Kids? A toxic relationship? Work stress?

How are you connecting to your body today? Or are you? What would reconnecting to your body look like? Remember, it doesn't have to be through barbells and burpees. That's just my story. It can be through anything, yoga, surfing, salsa dancing. It's whatever encourages you to start a new relationship with your body, one that you will continue to grow and nurture.

Motorcycles (My Spirit)

In the '80s, all the cool kids had dirt bikes. I really wanted a dirt bike. But my parents thought dirt bikes were too dangerous, so they bought me a 50cc Honda Spree scooter. Apparently they thought a little plastic motor scooter that required no helmet on the open road was safer than a motorcycle that was ridden only on dirt and required full gear head to toe. Anyway, I rode that little red death trap up and down the block every day for hours on end. It was the closest I felt to flying. Even when I was doing windmills (break-dancing), I didn't feel as free as I did on that scooter. It took away all my worries. My loneliness. I didn't care about anything else when I was on it. It gave me pure joy. It allowed the spirit of Chuck (my name then because the teachers couldn't pronounce my Korean name—Chul-Ki) to come out and play. It was more than a toy. It gave me an identity. It encapsulated who I was. Then I grew up and the Honda scooter turned into a Honda Civic. I was forced to bury the idea of ever feeling what I felt on two wheels when I was twelve. A small part of me died.

When I was married, I never considered having a motorcycle. My wife thought they were too dangerous, and I blindly agreed. The first thing I did after my divorce was buy a motorcycle. The Ducati Monster 620 Dark connected me to that twelve-year-old again. I rode that flat black open-engine motorcycle all over Ktown. Hugged canyons in Malibu. Took it to the beach. Drove it to coffee shops for my sessions with clients. I felt like Batman on that thing. It opened me up, connecting me to my truth—the spirit of Chuck (before my name was John), before taxes and marriage and all the shoulds. Before I began chasing things that weren't honest to me.

Since then, I've had five motorcycles. And every time I ride, I connect to the spirit of that little kid who zipped around the block wearing nothing but shorts, sandals, and a shit-eating grin. But it's not really about motorcycles. It's about this connection. My motorcycle is just a conduit that allows me to connect to that part of myself I once locked away because I had to "grow up." It makes me feel something when the rest of life makes me feel numb.

Now take a moment and ask yourself: How are you connecting to your spirit today? Or are you? When did you listen to your true spirit and allow it to dance? Or have you ever? What happened that killed your spirit? Choosing a career path you never wanted? Not giving yourself any time for yourself? Not doing things that are fun, that make you feel alive, that matter to you?

What would reconnecting to your spirit look like? It doesn't have to be with a Harley. Pick your poison—or more accurately, honey. I had a client who said he met God in the water so he picked up surfing again. And it doesn't have to be an activity, it can be creating a space. I have another client who completely redesigned his office his way, giving himself a creative space where his spirit could live—his spirit that he had locked away after becoming a CEO.

I had another client who said she felt the most alive in high school when she wore Doc Martens and carried drumsticks in her back pocket. She didn't even play drums. She carried drumsticks back then just because she liked them and didn't care what anyone else thought. For her, connecting to her true spirit now didn't mean strapping drumsticks to her MacBook on her way to work every day in the corporate world (though it could). But it did mean imagining the feeling of that wild and fearless high school girl who carried sticks in her back pocket and allowing that spirit to manifest in a way that was honest to her today. She started to care less what others thought, disengaged in gossip, and walked to the beat of her own drum (or imaginary drum in this case). When co-workers noticed that she was different, they wanted what she was having.

Reconnecting with your spirit can be anything that brings you back to yourself, that makes you feel alive and human. That allows the essence of you to shine.

Writing (My Soul)

I hated school. I didn't go to UCLA because I didn't apply. And I didn't apply because I knew I wouldn't get in. I was a C student, with SAT scores so low that the vice principal called me in and asked if "everything was okay at home." (I wonder if he would have asked me that if I weren't Asian.) I always felt like an idiot when it came to grades and education. I was the kid who was always looking out the window in science class, wondering what it would feel like to fly. Or have sex with my teacher. I was a dreamer. Still am.

I got a film degree because I loved movies. Most dreamers do. I chose my "emphasis in screenwriting" not because I wanted to be a screenwriter but because I had to make a choice: film production, film theory, or screenwriting. Screenwriting felt like the easiest. I never wanted to be a screenwriter. I just wanted to graduate.

After I failed as a screenwriter, I told myself I would never write again. I buried that part of me. For years, the only thing I wrote were case notes. I missed the days of turning words into life. Painting on paper. Then one day I decided to start a blog. I was in a dark place and just needed to express myself. I did it just for me, not for anyone else. Writing a blog was totally different from screenwriting. I wasn't writing to sell anything. I enjoyed the process because there was no pressure. Blogging made writing pure, and I slowly fell in love with it again. Since then, I have written over five thousand blog posts and three books (including this one).

I thought I had buried that part of myself because I had "failed" at it. But it never left. It never died. Once I started punching keys again, I realized that writing was a part of my soul. It was in my DNA. When I'm writing, I feel free. If I ignore it, I'm ignoring a core part of my identity. Ignoring my truth. It took being in a dark place—with myself and only myself—to connect back with writing.

I had a client once who felt depressed and lost. She was in her fifties. Superficially, nothing was wrong with her life. She just felt blah. I asked her when she had felt the most alive. In high school, she said. She had red rocker hair and played electric guitar. (Apparently I'm the therapist to see if you're a woman with a rock 'n' roll past?) She felt invincible then. She had fewer fucks to give. She liked herself. For homework, I told her to get a guitar. She didn't have to start playing it again. I just wanted her to pick one up and remember how it felt. So she went out and got an electric guitar. No, she didn't join a band or start playing every day again. But she played once in a while, and it sparked something. A feeling. It reminded her of who she really was.

We processed this. I asked her to describe the feeling. She said the guitar made her feel "heard, invincible, and a badass," like she felt roaming the empty hallways when she was supposed to be in class. Then I asked her: "In what areas of your life are you *not* feeling heard, invincible, or a badass?" All of them, she said. All areas of her life. Then the more important question: "How can you give yourself this feeling? What do you need to do to produce it?" We talked about her need to speak up at work and to express what she wanted in her relationship. To stop overextending herself with her friends and to meet them halfway instead. Maybe it was even time to find new friends and ditch old ones who were constantly taking from her.

Of course, this wouldn't be easy. But she got started, taking baby steps toward implementing these changes in her life. She slowly started to produce the feelings of being heard, feeling invincible, feeling like a badass. People on her team at work pushed back. They weren't used to hearing her speak up and voice her opinions. But her boss felt her newfound energy and loved it. Expressing what she needed in her relationship led to couples counseling, which she'd always wanted to do but was too afraid to suggest. And she lost some of her friends because they weren't used to this side of her. They said she had changed since she got "all zen and shit." But the truth was, they were not in a place themselves to change and grow, so they disappeared. She was totally okay with that.

This was the beginning of her journey back to self. It didn't follow a straight line pointed north. Like every journey, it zigzagged around. She found momentum, then snapped back, then made a few turns. But what's important is that she started on the journey. Because without going on a journey, you cannot come back to the village changed, with a new story you wrote yourself. Not the one written for you by someone else.

Like I said, connecting back to yourself isn't just about revisiting an activity you used to love. It's not about break-dancing per se, or riding a motorcycle, or picking up a guitar. It's about reconnecting with the spirit of the person you used to be when you liked yourself. Taking up an activity you gave up a long time ago can act as a vehicle for that reunion. But the reunion can also happen just by channeling the feeling of who you used to be and allowing that feeling to ripple through you, without having to know what that looks like. That feeling about yourself before all the realities of life got in the way. Before you had to take care of your parents. Before that toxic relationship. Before the kids. Before the all-consuming job. That feeling back when the world was big and open for adventure.

TIME TO MAKE SHIT HAPPEN

It's easier to love yourself than to like yourself. You can hide behind loving yourself. But you can't hide behind liking yourself. Loving yourself can be a box you check. Liking yourself requires a journey.

Do you like yourself? We're not talking about your nose or your butt. Do you like who you are at your core? If not, think about how you may have disconnected from your body, spirit, and soul. Why do you think that happened? What locked-away parts of yourself do you need to release in order to reconnect with yourself? Or maybe to establish a relationship with yourself for the first time?

Don't ask yourself when you were the happiest. That's too fucking broad. And "happy" can be a bumper sticker. Ask yourself when you felt most alive. It could be a moment, a year, or a period of your life. What was happening that made you feel this way? I felt the most alive when I was break-dancing. When I was riding that little red 50cc scooter. What about you? Maybe the time when you felt most alive wasn't during your childhood. Maybe it was just a few years ago. Think back and remember what that felt like. What can you do to regain that feeling?

Again, reconnecting with yourself is not about repeating an activity. It's about finding something that produces that same feeling so you can reconnect with your spirit. Something that can become a mindset or an intention. Because when we feel alive, we are connected to ourselves and our spirit. When we feel dead, we are not. Feed your spirit. But first, you need to find it. You need to embark on the journey.

What's one thing you can do this week to start this connection? What can you do at work? In your relationships? In your relationship with your body? Don't just write down ideas. Write down the actions you can take, and then execute them. Start the journey of liking yourself.

Self-Care
Is Your First Date

Self-care" has become one of those generic words that we see everywhere. All over social media, in books, on blogs, and in memes. People are wearing the SELF-CARE T-shirt but not actually practicing it. It's rarely on the top of their to-do list. Especially for men. *We don't need that shit.* It's at the bottom of the list with pedicures and massages. Too many men believe self-care is an extra, that men don't need self-care, that any man who practices self-care is weak. That's a false belief.

First, instead of theorizing about self-care, let's reexamine what it actually looks like in everyday life. Understand that self-care is different from self-love. If you're nowhere near a place of love for yourself, self-care can be a conduit to self-love. So stop telling yourself to love yourself. That's a loaded demand. There's pressure behind it. And it makes you feel defective if you struggle with it. The truth is, we all struggle with self-love because we don't know *how* to love ourselves. It's not something we practice. Yes, we're good at loving others. But rarely do we even prioritize loving ourselves, much less practice it.

So start small. Plan the first date with yourself and see where it goes.

Look, it doesn't have to be dinner and a movie. Or at the other extreme, a trip to Bali. That's self-help talk. A first date with yourself can be a walk. Or a workout. Or a cup of coffee sitting on a brick wall on a Saturday afternoon. It's not about the activity. It's about the connection. Are you connecting with yourself? Leaning into the discomfort of sitting with yourself? Or are you on your phone and in your head the entire time, running a to-do list or ruminating on why you haven't met someone? Can you give someone else your undivided attention? Do that for yourself.

Most people find it hard to pay attention to themselves. Because they haven't truly dated themselves. They've just done a lot of things alone, never particularly noticing how they felt. There's a huge difference. Like the difference between making love and fucking someone you barely know or like. The movements may be the same, but one experience connects you to yourself and builds self-esteem. The other disconnects you from yourself and drains your self-esteem.

Running to Stand Still

I was working in a nonprofit residential setting, counseling teenagers recovering from addiction. It was rewarding work but came with long hours and very little pay. One day after my shift I drove to the beach. Doing that was a bit left field for me. My life was about rebuilding now. It revolved around structure, daily routines, and getting shit done. I had so many case notes to catch up on, I was leading a family support program, and CrossFit class started in thirty minutes. I was on a strict program to transform my body and work toward licensure. No more dicking around. But not that day. Something hijacked me. I sat there alone on the sand on a random Tuesday staring at the sinking sun. Then the voices came. "What the fuck are you doing, you idiot! You're such a half-ass. You never finish anything. You want to be broke and working in nonprofit for the rest of your life?"

Suddenly I got up, smashed my towel into my backpack, and started running. Yes, running. I guess it was my way of stopping the voices. I ran down the shore, clenching the straps of my backpack as "Semi-Charmed Life" played on my iPod (hey, this was many moons ago). "I want something else. To get me through this, semi-charmed life." The song reminded me of beer bongs, getting hazed, and earthquakes. (I went to college in Northridge in the '90s.) I kept running and running. I kept waiting to get tired. But I didn't. I imagined I looked like a Korean Forrest Gump.

I passed a little girl chasing a seagull. We smiled when we made eye contact. When the waves washed up close to me, I didn't swerve around the water. Instead, I plowed through the waves like a soldier. People stared. I didn't give a fuck. I looked at surfers straddling their boards in the distance. I thought to myself, *How I wish I could surf*. Children threw sand at each other. A couple walked by, holding hands, triggering something in me—loneliness. Now I realized why I didn't want to go home.

I stayed at the beach all day. Then I bought myself an expensive meal on the pier. I thought about what I liked, what I didn't like, and all the different parts of myself I wanted to explore. I thought about what I wanted to do, and about some things I'd never thought about before. I laughed at myself for running on the beach and patted myself on the back for leaving work. I guess you can say it was my first true date. With myself.

Okay, is ditching work and running on the beach a form of self-care? Sure it is, if you are doing it to get to know yourself better, have a healthier relationship with yourself, and take care of yourself. But that wasn't why I was sprinting down the beach. I was already super-productive and taking care of myself on the outside through fitness classes and routines. But I was ignoring my emotional needs. I was mentally spent. I wasn't actually treating myself very well. I needed a reboot, a clearing. I needed sand in my toes and wind at my back. And also a fancy seafood dinner that I didn't know I needed. At least, I need it that day. And running allowed me to stop verbally bashing myself. I was treating myself well in action. You can call it self-care or dating yourself or being a little bitch (what the locker room has taught men to call it). Call it whatever you want. But simply put, I was building a relationship with me. For the first time in my life, I wasn't running.

Self-care doesn't mean bubble baths and fancy brunches. It really means taking care of yourself daily like you would for someone you love. It means breaking the pattern of putting yourself last. It means not taking on everything. Not overextending yourself. It means blowing out the candle when it's burning at both ends. It means saying no to things. It means considering your own needs, not over others' needs but *with* them, and meeting your needs.

And I get it. Self-care is hard. It's weird. You feel selfish and guilty doing it. You're not used to it. You've been programmed to take care of others and not yourself. And it's not like you'll wake up one day and suddenly love yourself after you decide to start practicing self-care. Yes, it starts with a decision, but it takes thousands of little actions, moments of tending to your needs, realizing that you matter and that it's your responsibility to take care of yourself if you want to be a better father, brother, husband, wife, teacher, artist, athlete, writer, or CEO. Self-care is a lifestyle. Not a checklist or a T-shirt.

Self-care is where a better you is born. It's your own soil for growth. It's not just for people who have extra time. Because the word "self-care" has been dipped in sugar and slapped on memes, it can make us cringe a bit. Like the movie everyone keeps telling us to see so much that we don't really want to see it anymore. So for now, forget about the words "self-care" and "loving yourself." Instead, think of it as connecting to yourself or disconnecting from yourself. If you start building a better relationship with yourself by giving yourself what you need and treating yourself better, in your actions, words, thoughts, and intentional practice of self-care, you are connecting to yourself. If you're not, you are disconnecting from yourself. When you connect, your potential grows. When you disconnect, your potential shrinks. It's that simple. Self-care is connecting to self. No self-care is disconnecting from self.

Here are some questions that can help you start the process: How is your relationship with yourself these days? Forget about loving yourself. Do you even like yourself? If not, why? What happened? Is there something you need to let go of or accept? Do you need to forgive yourself for something? Do you need to cut the bond keeping what you do tied up with what you're worth? Are you answering honestly?

What would be different in your life if you got to a place where you actually liked yourself? Where you weren't forced to like yourself, but genuinely liked yourself? Would liking yourself impact the people you choose to surround yourself with? The person you choose to love? Let me ask you something else. What does it take to actually like someone, to think of them as one of your favorite people? It takes time, right? You have to get to know that other person. Have you been taking the time to get to know yourself these days? Or did that stop when life happened? What would it look like to get to know yourself again?

Okay, now forget about liking yourself. Because that takes time. You'll work on it. What about love? Love is a choice. How do you like to be loved by someone? At the end of the day, to love someone means to respect them, treat them well, allow them to be heard, validate and support them, and champion their story. Right? Not just in action but also in words. Actions and words go hand in hand. If someone treats you well but speaks to you like shit, that's not love. Or if someone speaks to you with love and kindness but treats you like shit, that's not love. It comes down to actions and words, and they should line up. That's how you love someone. Anything else isn't love. And if it's not love, there is no way to build a healthy relationship. Sound familiar?

Can you love yourself the way you would like someone to love you and the way you love others? You might not have practiced it enough. It's probably not something you consciously put effort into or think about when you're going about your day. Well, it's time to start.

Remember, self-care is *not* just a coping method. It's a way of connecting. To you.

Let's bring it down to street level:

Connecting to yourself through self-care can mean treating yourself to a doughnut once in a while. Going home early on a Friday. Drawing healthy boundaries with friends, family, co-workers. Speaking up at work. Taking the motorcycle instead of the car. Therapy. Getting a babysitter so you can paint. Not your house but on canvas, to feed that creative need that's a part of you and you've been ignoring for so long.

Self-care could mean telling yourself you matter. Acknowledging how far you've come and who you are today because of it. Not bashing yourself every time you "fuck up." Practicing self-compassion and forgiveness, which, by the way, is a daily choice. Being easier on yourself. Giving yourself space to be human. Self-care is building a better relationship with yourself by listening to yourself and giving yourself what you need and deserve.

Every relationship requires you to look inward, to examine where your feelings are coming from and why. To take ownership and change patterns. To learn where the cracks in your pavement are. Any relationship—including the one you have with yourself—is a process of discovery. Your relationship with yourself is a daily practice, and as in every relationship, some days are going to be easy and some days are going to feel impossible. That's where self-compassion comes in. You have to be compassionate toward yourself, just as you would practice compassion when your partner is not being their best self. But you also have to call yourself out, as you would your partner. Know when you're hiding and not being honest with yourself. This is what working on a relationship with you looks like.

First, ask yourself how you treat and speak to the people you love.

I'll go first.

When it comes to the people I love in my life—my friends, family, and partner—I treat them with respect. I try to provide a safe space for them to be heard. I champion their story. I accept them and their shortcomings. I practice empathy and compassion. I consider their entire story and try not to judge. I am supportive. I am accepting. I encourage their dreams. I am understanding. I talk to them with kindness. I don't assassinate their character. I listen. I give them the benefit of the doubt. I truly want the best for them.

Now flip it back on me. Do I treat and talk to myself the same way? Of course not. I am much harder on myself. I talk to myself in a way that I would never do with others. I bash myself. I put undue pressure on myself. I hold myself to a higher standard than I do others. I put shitty food in my body and then shame myself for it. I don't treat or talk to myself like I do in my other relationships.

Now ask yourself: In what ways are you not treating yourself the way you treat the people you love? How is your current relationship with yourself? How are you treating yourself (action)? And how are you talking to yourself (words)? Are you bashing yourself? Are you assassinating your own character and calling yourself fat, stupid, lazy? How you talk to yourself is actually more important than how you treat yourself. Because how you talk to yourself will determine how you treat yourself. Words turn into actions more easily than actions turn into words.

All those ways in which you're not supporting and speaking to yourself are the ways you should support and speak to the people you love. That's what you need to work on.

Pump These Pistons or Your Life Engine Will Not Move

L et's break down the relationship you have with yourself into three simple categories: your body, your mind, and your soul. To have a better relationship with yourself, start by feeding and connecting to these three areas. Imagine your mind, body, and soul as the pistons of an engine. They all need to pump together in order for the engine to move forward. If one piston is off, the engine is stuck. But if they all have what they need, then the engine moves forward. And if you do this long enough, that's when things will really rev up. You literally become a well-oiled machine. And you start to like yourself.

Let's tackle each category.

How Are You Treating Your Body?

Your body is not a temple. Stop thinking of it as so precious and delicate. It's moldable, adjustable, and stretchable. It's meant to be broken down to grow back stronger. We're meant to move. Every. Single. Day. (A big shout-out to rest days and listening to your body and knowing how much to push it and not. But I am front-loading the message about moving every day because most of us don't move enough.)

Instead of pushing ourselves, we find excuses. We get lazy. Until we catch a glimpse of ourselves in the mirror and realize we really need to do something. Or we have that moment lying in bed after mechanical sex when we realize that our unhealthy relationship with our body affects not only our own life but the life of our partner and the intimacy of our life together. That's when we draw the line. We go on extreme diets and detoxes and put ourselves through rigorous workouts that make us curse the day we were born. Because we feel like we *have* to. And whenever we feel like we *have* to do something, it never lasts. We keep putting Band-Aids on the problem instead of finding true healing, growth, and transformation.

Here's the thing. What's needed isn't getting motivated to exercise or finding the perfect diet. What's needed is building a better relationship with our bodies. We don't take care of our bodies because we have a poor relationship with them. We don't value our bodies for the miraculous machines they are. Instead, we push them away, reject them, detach ourselves from them. Or on the other extreme, we see our body only in relation to our sex appeal. We measure our worth by the shape of our back, butt, and legs.

Either of these views of the body is a form of disconnecting from yourself. That's why your relationship with your body is the most important. A healthy relationship with your body will give you balance and permission to be yourself. The relationship isn't contingent on how you look, and you don't slide into a well of shame when you think you don't measure up. You don't feel forced to exercise and to eat well. Regular exercise and good nutrition are the by-products of the healthy relationship you've built with yourself. Instead of yo-yoing, you have a relationship with your body that's sustainable and steady.

It's time to focus on building a better relationship with your body. So how does treating your body better become a daily way of life instead of a daily struggle?

STEP 1: ACCEPT YOUR BODY

Everything starts with acceptance. This is true about all aspects of life, including your relationship with your body. Wherever you're at is where you're at. This doesn't mean you don't want to change your body. It just means that your body is your body and you are accepting it as yours. No more rejecting it. No more hating it. No more wishing you had someone else's body.

Everyone has insecurities about their body. If they say they don't, they're either lying or have never been exposed to any advertising. I have many insecurities. I wish I was a few inches taller. I wish I could get rid of the pudge around my waist. My legs are too short. My wrists are too skinny. My nose is too wide. And on and on and on. But I've accepted my body. It is mine. I can work with it. And there are parts of it I can change. I can build a better body, a stronger body, but only if I accept it first. Everything starts there.

STEP 2: DROP INTO YOUR BODY

Notice, feel, and be in your body.

Most people see their own bodies from outside of themselves, especially women, so let's start with them. As a woman, you learn at an early age that your body holds some sort of external worth. When you were a girl, you compared your body to the girls who developed faster and thought something was wrong with you. You noticed the attention they were getting and could see that you weren't getting it. You believed you were less than. Or you developed too fast and didn't like the attention you got so you covered up your body. Hid it. Hated it. Your body drew attention, the kind you didn't want or weren't ready for. Add to this the constant pressures from magazines, ads, and insensitive partners, drilling into your head what "beauty" looked like. You may have thought your own idea of beauty was based on your "preferences," but those preferences developed from exposure to the distorted images of beauty in the media, magazines, porn, or whatever else you were exposed to. Everywhere you go, everything you see, there is pressure to look a certain way. No wonder so many women have body dysmorphia and develop eating disorders. They can never fulfill the unrealistic expectations bombarding them. It's really easy to feel ugly in our world.

Responding to these pressures, you come to see your body as an object, as something outside of yourself. It's there to call attention, either positive or negative. So you are always on alert, in self-protection mode. Always looking over your shoulder. Being aware of your space and boundaries. Deflecting inappropriate stares. You are subtly or not so subtly in a constant state of fight-or-flight, which prevents you from connecting to your body. Your body is no longer a friend. It is the enemy.

Men also define themselves by their bodies. It starts with idolizing superheroes, and that follows us into locker rooms and onto the football field, the basketball court, the baseball diamond. If we don't have muscles, we are seen as weak. Or maybe it's not physical strength we lack but physical ability. We notice the attention boys get when they can skate, surf, throw, tackle. If we don't have these abilities, we are the last one picked for teams. And we internalize a belief that our lack of physical ability makes us less than.

No, we don't get as much pressure from society and advertising as women do. But we do get it from other men. And from porn. We internalize the images and expectations about penis size, performance, body types. Porn stars used to be chubby with mustaches. Now they look like abnormally endowed quarterbacks. This brainwashing pollutes our sense of worth as well as our relationships, hurting the people we care about the most. Let's take a detour to see what this looks like in real life.

Even Wonder Woman
Has to Take Her Bracelets
Off Sometimes

Anna was a phenomenal athlete. She did Cross-Fit competitions, Spartan races, and triathlons. Her body was a fucking machine. She was also a mother, wife, and CrossFit Box owner who had built an amazing community. Everyone saw her as Wonder Woman. She was hardworking and humble, and she gave back to her community.

She came in to see me as what I call a "single-serving" client—a client who wants just one session. Or in Anna's case, a "tune-up." She said there was nothing wrong with her life. She just wanted to make sure she was mentally sound. The CrossFit Open, an annual global fitness competition, was coming up, and she wanted to make sure her head was straight.

But then, as we started to talk about her life, she broke down. She admitted that she wasn't happy. On paper, things were great. There were no "holes" in her life. She had a solid relationship with her husband. Her daughter was "becoming a little beautiful human." She loved her job. She had great friends. Nothing was wrong. But she felt empty and couldn't understand why. After many sessions (because no one is ever really a single-serving client), she realized that she was completely disconnected from her body.

We might think that no population is more connected to their bodies than athletes. I certainly thought so. But for Anna, it wasn't true. She saw her body as a machine, as something outside of herself. A vehicle, or a separate container. A tool to accomplish things with. And of course, this view disconnected her from herself because it prevented her from actually dropping into her body. For her, there was no oneness of body and mind and soul because she didn't listen to her body. Her body listened to her. And yes, measuring only her performance, that produced amazing fitness results. But in severing her connection with herself, she had created a toxic relationship with herself.

This divide between Anna and her body started when she was in high school. She wasn't a track all-star or the captain of the swim team. In fact, she didn't play sports at all. She was actually underweight and struggled with an eating disorder. Her home life was chaotic, and food was the only thing she could control. Then, as she grew up, the pendulum swung the other way, from starving herself to overexercising. From the outside, it looks like she had overcome her eating disorder and become an amazing athlete. She genuinely believed this herself. But in our sessions she realized that her internal process had not changed. She still struggled with expressing her feelings, with all-or-nothing thinking, and with extreme behavior—all the same struggles she'd had in high school. Her unhappiness was coming from the same issues she'd always had.

She decided to skip the CrossFit Open that year. Wonder Woman took off her bracelets. It was one of the most difficult decisions she had ever made. She had to deal with not only her disappointment over skipping the competition but also her feeling that she was letting down her community— and letting go of her identity in the process. But if she didn't get honest with herself, she would be a fraud.

So Anna started a brand-new relationship with her body. For the first time in her life, she actually dropped into her body. She listened to it instead of telling it what to do. She allowed herself to feel her feelings for the first time in her life, and she began to express them as well. It was hard for her to fight years of programming, but she approached dropping into her body like training—emotional training instead of physical training.

When she told her community and her husband what she was doing, they all supported her. The more she connected, accepted, and dropped into her body, the happier she became. The pressure to be a superhero was gone, and the giant weight she'd been carrying since age fifteen was lifted off her. People loved and looked up to Anna for being Anna, not what her body could do. Wonder Woman realized she didn't need the bracelets after all.

Dropping into your body is the process of becoming a whole person. It's accepting yourself in action. You can't know yourself if you don't drop into your body. It's your body that has the answers, not your mind.

As a daily practice, notice the feeling of your bare feet as they touch the floor in the morning. The weight of your body as you stand. The crack of your bones. The strength of your spine. Notice how your body feels under cold water. Or under warm water. Notice your breath, and how your body feels when you focus on it. Notice the tightness in your body. Notice the looseness.

Feel the hot coffee going down your throat and notice how that makes your body feel. Notice your grip on the steering wheel. Notice sensations in your body as you listen to music or a podcast. Or when someone cuts you off. Notice where your mind goes when you sit in rush hour traffic, but more important, notice how each thought makes your body feel.

Notice your body as you engage with different people throughout the day. Who makes you tense? Why is that? Who calms you? What is it about them that's soothing? Notice the energy of others and the way you feel their energy in your body. Notice your own energy when you laugh, shaping the lines of your face. What happens when you feel stressed. What happens when the afternoon slump comes and your eyelids get heavy. Notice the tastes in your mouth when you eat your lunch. Notice how your body feels if you eat fast. Notice the bloating in your stomach. Or the relief of the bloat going away. Notice how your body feels during certain conversations.

Feel your body as you pedal your bike or do a burpee or push into a downward dog. Feel your legs. Your arms. Your joints. Feel the stretching of your back. Notice how your body feels as you start to sweat and it gets harder and harder to breathe. Notice where your body tightens. Where it feels good. Notice how your body feels after the workout. Feel the heat radiating off your neck. Notice how you walk. Are you taller? Does your body feel lighter? Do you feel stronger?

Does anyone really do this? Of course not. Mainly because we're thinking all the time. I mean, who's got the time to notice how they feel in their body every minute of the day? But if you don't make an effort to do just that, you will always be disconnected from your body. Living in your head and leading with logic prevents you from being present. The here and now is where life is lived, and the way to get there is through your body, not your mind. You can't think life. You live it by feeling it. To reconnect with your body, you have to reset your default from thinking to being. As a daily practice. It may feel awkward at first because you're not used to it. After all, you're changing years and years of wiring. But through practice, being instead of thinking will get easier.

If you don't drop into your body, you can't be in touch with what it's trying to tell you. You won't be in tune with the feeling you get when you know you're making the wrong decision. Or when you're making the right one. You won't fully feel how another person makes you feel. You won't feel what you want or don't want. Your body is a radar system that guides you on your journey. It's where your intuition, soul, and truth live. If you don't drop into your body, accept it, listen to it, and feel it, you will not know yourself, or like yourself. You will make decisions that are not honest to you. You'll become a walking shell.

Move with Your Body

You build a healthy relationship with your body by accepting it, dropping into it, and listening to it. But that's just the beginning. The relationship with your body is also built by moving with it, stretching it, pushing it past what you think it's capable of. That journey produces confidence and new beliefs about what you can do. You can say, well, Anna moved her body a lot. Yes, but did she move *with* her body or did she just move it? There is a huge difference. Only one leads to a connection to self.

What's the difference between moving your body and moving with your body? You're moving with your body when you're doing things that your body enjoys and also needs. When you're not moving in a certain way because it's popular, or because you just want to look better naked. Moving in ways your body enjoys and needs could mean switching up your fitness by doing different things, or switching up your diet by eating different foods, depending on what your body wants and needs. Only you know your relationship with your body, so you have to be really honest with yourself.

Also, it's not just about movement outside the house. It's about moving with your body in the bedroom too. Are you just moving your body during sex, or moving only for your partner? Or are you moving *with* your body? Moving to give your body what it wants and needs? Is sex mechanical and predictable? Are you moving your body the same way you've done since high school? Are you moving it in a way you think your partner wants, or moving in a way that feels good to you? Are you just going through the motions? Or are you fulfilling your sexual needs and desires by listening to what your body wants, desires, and craves? This isn't just about better sex. It's about a better connection. With yourself first, and then with someone else.

When I was younger, I moved with my body when I was break-dancing or skateboarding. Then, in my twenties, I spent a lot of time just moving my body at the gym. I did that purely for aesthetic reasons. I was completely disconnected from my body and just wanted to look good. Then, in my thirties, as I was going through my rebirth, I found CrossFit and got obsessed with it. For the first time in a long time, I was moving with my body again. It made me feel alive and connected me to that twelve-year-old who spun on his head every day after school.

CrossFitting was pretty much all I did for nearly a decade. When I began, I was moving with my body. But after a decade, I was just moving my body. My body was craving something new and different, but I didn't listen to it. Until recently. Today I still do CrossFit, but only once or twice a week. I also take sprint class, do yoga once in a while, hike, do strength training, and swim when I can. I also ride my motorcycle almost every day, which I consider moving with my body since it connects me to myself.

The activity doesn't matter. What matters is that you listen to and connect with your body through movement. You have to enjoy the movement. If you don't, you won't connect. You will just be going through the motions. That said, you have to challenge yourself and do some exploring. And in order to explore, you have to push past discomfort and try new things. You can't eat the same thing your entire life and expect to find the same enjoyment in it day in and day out. Never changing the menu may be comfortable, but even comfortable can feel empty. Enjoyment is there to be found and discovered. It lives past the breakers, and you have to swim out there to find it. It's in the swimming that you will find new connections and establish a new relationship with your body. You will believe you can do something different, that you're actually good at something you didn't know you could be good at. This will shift your beliefs, bolster your self-worth, and, most important, connect you back to yourself.

You establish a healthier relationship with your body by accepting it, dropping into it, and moving with it. Not once, but as a lifestyle.

How to Treat
Your Mind Better

According to neuroscience expert and bestselling author Dr. Joe Dispenza, we have approximately sixty thousand thoughts a day. Most of those thoughts not only are negative but are the same thoughts we had yesterday. So besides swimming in our own shit, we are also living in the past. Really think about this. It's a game-changer. The same thoughts produce the same feelings, which produce the same behavior, which leads to the same experiences. And I'll take this one step further. Having the same experiences cements the same false beliefs. Basically, we live in a loop—a pattern that keeps us stuck and disconnected, not only from ourselves but also from the world.

Most of us treat our minds poorly by allowing this loop to continue uninterrupted, sinking us deeper and deeper into our own mental quicksand. It will keep being our natural default unless we do something about it. But before I get into the steps you can take to treat your mind better and pull yourself out of your mental quicksand, I want to point something out that you may not have thought about before. It has helped me tremendously. It's this one fact: those negative voices don't belong to you.

Mom, You Won the Fucking Lottery!

As I was connecting more to myself, I felt I should also connect more to my family. Let me rephrase that: as I was connecting more to myself, I felt I had more tools to connect to my family. My parents lived only twenty minutes from me, and yet I never saw them. So I decided to make an effort. I was a new man now. We would meet once a month at a Sizzler in Glendale. I don't know what it is about Sizzlers, but Koreans love them.

The first time I sat down with my parents, a panic set in, as if I'd been plunged in an ice bath. But I had decided to use them as an exercise in learning how not to get snapped back to the old reactive John Kim. I had an idea. I wanted to try something new. I decided to ask my mom a fun question, like a "would you rather . . ." question before my dad had a chance to pummel me with an hour of continuous nagging followed by a "sell your motorcycle and here's what you need to do with your life" speech. I asked my mom what she would do if she won the lottery. I know, the most generic question on the planet. But you have to remember, I don't speak much Korean and they don't speak much English, so we're all talking on a sixth-grade level here.

My mom's first response was to complain about how much she has to pay in taxes. And that's when it hit me. There's no way my even-keeled, rarely excited about good news attitude, my glass-is-not-only-half-empty-but-cracked-and-stupid thinking, is just me. I think that way in large part because I learned to. It was passed down from my parents, from my upbringing, and from the environment I grew up in. I grew up in a house of panic: all we cared about was how much fried chicken we sold (we owned a Popeye's Chicken). Life was black or white. Good if we sold a lot of chicken. Bad if we didn't. And yeah, I get it. My parents grew up in poverty and their mental dials are permanently set on survival. But now I knew mine didn't have to be.

Now I can think back on moments with my parents and understand that the negative voice in my head developed over time, and that it was passed down to me from them. Here are some actual conversations we had—the way I remember them anyway.

ONE SIZZLER CONVERSATION

John and his parents are having their monthly catch-up. His parents are enjoying the all-you-can-eat salad bar. John is not eating.

MOM
You like nerds?

JOHN
What?

MOM
Nerds. You like nerds?

JOHN
You mean like the candy?

MOM
What candy?

JOHN
What the hell are you talking about?

MOM
Dad went to hospital and found beautiful nerds.

JOHN
You mean nurse!

MOM
Ya.

JOHN
I'm not going on a date with someone Dad found at a hospital.

MOM
She work there. No patient. She nurse.

JOHN
So?

MOM
So she take care of you.

JOHN
I don't need anyone to take care of me.

MOM
What if you hurt?

JOHN
I have insurance.

MOM
She want to meet you.

JOHN

You told her I was a doctor, didn't you?

MOM

Dad say.

JOHN

I am not a doctor! I am a therapist. I'm not even a therapist. I'm a therapist in training.

DAD (*eating a roll*)

Same thing.

ANOTHER SIZZLER CONVERSATION

John and his parents are having their monthly catch-up. His parents are enjoying the all-you-can-eat salad bar. John is not eating.

DAD

You date somebody?

JOHN

I'm dating myself.

DAD

What, you gay?

JOHN

No, I'm growing.

DAD

You forty year old. No more growing. Impossible.

JOHN

Thirty-seven.

MOM

You have to make baby.

JOHN

What if I don't want to?

MOM

You have to. Only way be happy.

JOHN

You mean it's the only way *you'll* be happy.

DAD

Doctor say I die five year.

JOHN

You said that five years ago.

DAD

New doctor.

I started thinking about all the external influences on my thoughts and ways of thinking. I thought about the blueprints I was following and whether they were honest to me (more about this in Act II). Although our thoughts are our own, they have been influenced by teachers, parents, boyfriends, girlfriends, and unhealthy experiences. We acquire desires that don't even belong to us. Realizing this felt like a huge weight being lifted. It made me understand that *I* wasn't at fault. That I'm not defective. That I am a product of where I grew up, who raised me, and what has happened to me. And I realized I could return that shit and think new thoughts, choose my own ways of thinking.

How to Do Better

STEP 1: AWARENESS—SHINE A BLACK LIGHT ON YOUR THOUGHTS

Most of us don't think about how we think. Most of us don't shine a black light on our daily thoughts. We just allow them in and we can drown in them. Sometimes they consume us, control us, making us tense and anxious, keeping us in a panic state. When this happens, we're pulled out of the present and start to live in our heads (in the past or in the future). That is not actually living. It's just worrying a lot.

Step 1 is to become aware of this. Notice your thoughts. Don't judge them. Just practice noticing them. Also, notice the feeling in your body when you have those thoughts. Notice. Notice. Notice. Watch your thoughts as if they were drifting in a snow globe.

STEP 2: QUESTION YOUR THOUGHTS

Many of our thoughts are marked by faulty logic and stem from fear. We dwell on the past and worry about the future. We exaggerate, jump to conclusions, and play back memories through the old lens of who we used to be. We create stories because we are afraid. Over and over and over again. Until these kinds of thoughts become our default, our knee-jerk way of thinking. Thinking this way becomes more than a habit. It becomes a way of living. Or actually, not living. All we're doing is waking up, drinking too much caffeine, and doing lots and lots of thinking.

Break this pattern by questioning your thoughts. Is there truth in them or are they tainted? Put your thoughts on trial.

Know that thoughts are not facts. They're just thoughts. They will come and go. Don't get attached to them and allow them to get so heavy and negative that they drown you.

STEP 3: NOTICE RECURRING PATTERNS IN YOUR THOUGHTS

Can you discern patterns in your way of thinking? Do you jump to conclusions? Do you struggle with all-or-nothing thinking? Do you assume that another person is thinking something about you when they're not? What are the circumstances when you do that? What feelings trigger this type of thinking? And more important, how do the patterns distorting your thinking manifest in your behavior? Do you break up with your partner because they forgot to text you within an hour? Do you sabotage opportunities because you don't think you can do something without any real proof that you can't? Do you try to fix things for people who didn't ask you to just so you can believe you are valuable?

Treating your mind better means understanding how it works. Once you start to understand how your thinking affects your behavior, you can take action to correct both your thought patterns and your behavior. Everything starts with understanding. Without it, you will just go through a lot of motions. Once you really understand your patterns and their impact on your everyday life and choices, you will know what you need to work on.

After you do these three steps—becoming aware of your thoughts, questioning your thoughts, and finding the patterns in your thoughts—you'll be able to pull back and see what's going on. You'll no longer believe that bad things happen because you're unlucky or defective. You'll understand that this thought is distorted and a reaction to false beliefs about yourself. Once you see the process, you can choose to fix it by stopping it. When you notice your distorted thinking or false beliefs or fear, instead of reacting, you can evaluate. You now know that there is a different path and you can choose to take it by responding differently. By doing so, you give yourself a new experience, and the more new experiences you give yourself, the more you create new tracks.

You know that eating a healthy diet and getting regular exercise can transform your body. The hard part, of course, is actually *doing* those things. It's the same with transforming your ingrained thoughts, distorted thinking, and false beliefs. Those old habits of thought run deep, and you can't change them just by reading something or willing them to change. As I mentioned earlier, transformation takes a daily practice. The goal is to get to a place where you start to notice a difference. And you have to believe that your new practice will work or you won't do it.

Detach to Connect

We don't just have one isolated thought many times. Our thoughts come in series. They are episodic. They tell stories that take us down dark slippery wells we can't climb out of. We ruminate by playing the same thoughts, the same stories, over and over, like broken records. Our world gets very small as we live in these trenches. We can't see anything besides the mental exaggerations we project from faulty thinking. We can't see truth, or what could be. Instead, we see only what was and what can't be. Do this long enough and you start to lose hope. The sky turns gray. You wonder why you get up every day. Feeling hopeless without relief is the fastest route to depression.

But there is hope. You can take a breath and a giant step back. You can observe yourself, detach from your thoughts, and create a space for revelations. Detaching from your faulty thoughts is actually a great way of connecting back to yourself. Once you create distance, you can observe and get a more accurate picture of how you work. You can see the truth, undistorted by negative thoughts and faulty thinking.

This is why meditation is so big these days in Western culture (the East has been on to it for ages). Meditation creates this space. This practice allows you to release thoughts that once hooked you. Now, instead of reacting to your thoughts, you can let them float by. You can let go and choose to respond (the power-filled choice) instead of react (the powerless choice). It's the difference between being in the eye of a tornado, where it's calm and you can see what's going on, or being on the edge of the tornado, where you are spun around and around like a rag doll. By detaching from your thoughts as a practice, as a lifestyle, you can live in the eye.

Once you get this distance on your thoughts, you can see yourself as an experiment. You can notice things instead of judging them. This is where you can really get traction.

My First Sweat Angel

By now, I had been CrossFitting for about a year. I was ready to push myself and tackle workouts that were more like events. Like belts in martial arts, these workouts test your fitness by your score. You keep that score (belt) until the next time the workout comes up. One of these workouts, called "Fight Gone Bad," was made for MMA fighter B. J. Penn as a simulation of what it would feel like after a fight. The movements include wall balls, push presses, rowing, box jumps, and sumo dead lifts. The weight is fairly light, but you're going balls to the wall (pun intended). Each rep is a point, and the goal is to get as many points as you can in less than a certain amount of time. Anything north of 350 is a really great score. At my CrossFit facility, that would put you in the top five. So that was my target to shoot for.

It didn't feel like a fight to me. It felt like getting jumped by a gang. The first round was nothing but panic and fear. The second round hit, and I questioned everything. I think I was even questioning why I came to this country. Then, somewhere in the third round, I left my mind and dropped into my body. I detached from all my negative thoughts and thought patterns. I started focusing on the feeling of the movements and moving through them like a dance. I was out of my head and in my body.

They say your mind stops you way before your body does. This means you can always push yourself physically much further than you think you can. Dropping into your body, you can hit a flow state and perform at your optimal level. When athletes set world records, I can promise you that they're not thinking about their taxes or the fight they had with their girlfriend the night before. They are not thinking about anything. They are detached, fully engaged and present.

That day I didn't let my mind stop me. I detached from it.

I always sweat when I do a CrossFit workout, dripping like I pissed my pants, but that was the first time I actually left a sweat angel on the floor. I believe my score was around 300. But that wasn't the win. The big win for me was the revelation on the drive home. If you see yourself as an experiment and distance yourself from your thinking so you stop allowing your thoughts to have power over you, you can do more than you believe you can.

Food for Thought—Feed Your Brain

How we treat our minds isn't just about changing our thoughts and how we think. In today's world, our minds have to deal with more noise than ever before. And it's coming at us from all angles, at all times. Our world rains information. Clickbait has become the new entertainment, whether it takes us to a controversial blog post, a shocking video, or even a funny cat video. Because one funny cat video turns into fifty, and suddenly we've wasted two hours of our life. And this doesn't just happen now and then. It's become a daily habit. Clickbait gives us a dopamine surge by making us laugh or entertaining us with the same rush we get from horror movies. But these aren't movies. These videos are showing us real life. For that reason, you may not see the habit as being as damaging as binging on television. But it's just as bad as TV, if not worse, because it's everywhere and it never ends. Death by a thousand paper cuts.

Your mind is just as important as your stomach. If you feed it shit, you will feel shitty. Treat your mind well by feeding it good things. It's time to consume what will enrich you as an individual.

Let's break it down.

THE INTERNET AND SOCIAL MEDIA

The internet and social media can be amazing tools to build a more potent version of yourself. But you have to put intention behind your use of these tools. You can't just scroll and post what you're eating. Use social media as a tool to share your story and find your voice. Use it to practice vulnerability. To show yourself. Decide what you feel comfortable sharing and what you're not going to share. But also be courageous: when others relate to your story, your story becomes bigger than you. By sharing it, you are accepting your story instead of ripping out chapters you don't like. Sharing your story is empowering, a way to connect you back to yourself, to accept yourself.

Use social media to find communities and create a dialogue on something you're passionate about. There are real people with real stories behind those profiles. Use social media to find your tribe and feel less alone in the world. But be picky about who and what you follow. It's easy to zone out on pointless content and participate in gossip. It's easy to drown in the negativity online, both the content and the comments people leave. The negativity can take you hostage and make you see the world as worse than it is. Remember, whatever you feed will grow. If you watch nothing but what's wrong in the world, you will not want to leave your house or have children.

PODCASTS

Podcasts are the new radio. Pick a podcast that stimulates your brain, with episodes that create a dialogue about topics you're passionate about. That make you think, inspire and motivate you, make you a smarter, better human. We learn through our stories. Listen to amazing stories from amazing people. Nothing is more inspiring than a person's character arc. Listen to your favorite stories and you will realize that you have a character arc as well. Knowing this means you're going somewhere. You matter. You have a story like everyone you're listening to on podcasts. Maybe start your own podcast.

AUDIOBOOKS

Confession: I don't read. I'm not sure if it's ADD or what, but after about ten pages of reading anything, I zone out.

It's always been a problem, and an embarrassing one. Thank God for the invention of the audiobook. Because I can listen well. Anything I listen to sticks. Probably because I'm a therapist. So I take in a book or two a week. I listen mostly to self-betterment and philosophy but other topics as well, from relationships to sexuality to spirituality to mindfulness to addiction to mindset to logistical topics like structuring your day. It depends on where I'm at in my life and what I feel I need to learn. I listen to anything that will help me know myself better, juggling a couple of audiobooks at a time.

Just Googling shit on the internet isn't as powerful as reading or listening to books. Books are more than information. They have stories, voice, and perspective. They are personal and will leave a much greater imprint than Google ever will. I've learned more from audiobooks than from all my traditional school education combined. They've really changed my life. Now I feed my brain by "reading" constantly.

You connect to yourself by treating your mind better. Thread books, audio or print, into your daily life. Books make you better. I promise.

Finding My Soul While Shitting in the Woods

**The desire to know your soul
will end all other desires.**

—RUMI

You're feeding your mind now. Are you also feeding your soul? Are you listening to it? Respecting it? Giving it what it needs? Have you ever? I hadn't until I was thirty-five. I didn't even know I had a soul. This is the most important piece. Why? Because the soul is the part of us that we forget. Mind and body come together, a package deal. But we don't think about our soul. We leave it on a shelf somewhere. We ignore it because we think it's extra, something we will feed when we become "successful." What we don't realize is that failing to feed our soul prevents us from truly becoming.

———

He swung like Tarzan on crack as he leaped into the lake. Popped his head up from under the water and yelled, "It's warm. Feels amazing!" I was next in line. The rope swung toward me as if it were a vine from God. I grabbed onto it for dear life and flew out over the water like a sideways monkey, realizing quickly the fucker was lying. The water was ice cold! I tasted my testicles as they shot up into my mouth. I screamed as I dog-paddled toward the rocks, where twelve other men were peeling off their dirt bike gear to take their turn, and I felt a kind of love I hadn't in a long time. You see, this prank had to be earned, or it would have just been annoying instead of an expression of bonding. It had taken seven days in the woods, campfires, dirt bikes, and dudes being their authentic selves, without posturing or trying to prove anything, to earn it.

I didn't grow up like other kids. I didn't have a dad who took me fishing and camping. I never joined the Boy Scouts, never learned how to tie ropes and make fires. My parents were always at work. I grew up on concrete. Skateboarding and spinning on my head. I'm afraid of the wilderness. I'm terrified of animals. I've only gone camping twice and brought a hair dryer both times. So when my friend invited me to go camping for seven days, I felt instant resistance. Normally, I would have declined, but it was his bachelor party. I couldn't say no. We rode from Sequoia to Yosemite on dirt bikes and camped under the stars. It was my first man trip and the first time I'd been on a dirt bike.

It didn't hit me until the very end of the trip. We were coming out of a long tunnel after hundreds of miles of riding over rocks, water, and fallen trees. Our bones were aching. Our bodies were tired, and our eyes crusted with dirt. At the end of the tunnel was the entrance to Yosemite. The finish line. As we were coming out of the tunnel, we saw an older Asian man on the side of the road, standing on a rock and waving an American flag at us. It was very strange, almost as if he knew we were coming. Everything went into slow motion. (Literally too: Google "Makes you better Yosemite moto" and you'll see the actual video footage.) He reminded me of my dad, who had recently passed.

My dad came to this country with two sons, a wife, five hundred bucks, and a relentless passion to live the American Dream. But all he did in America was work, pulling telephone cable. Yeah, he had some buddies he'd play pool and drink soju with. But he did nothing to feed his soul. There was no such thing as self-care in his life. He just grinded. Just like my mom. At least he had friends. My mom never had any friends. She just worked and made sure her sons had cool shit so they wouldn't get made fun of at school.

My dad pulled telephone cable his entire American life. My mom flipped burgers and fried chicken. Maybe that's why "soul" wasn't in my vocabulary. It was a foreign concept. I'd never seen it in action. At least not in my family. My parents followed that waving flag here. America meant something to them. It was the island to swim to, the pot of gold at the end of a long rainbow. But I don't believe they ever found it. Because the gold is not at the end. It's sprinkled throughout the rainbow, and if you don't feed your soul, you never see it. That's what hit me as I watched that Asian man waving that flag. Maybe it was a caution sign.

All of us on that trip were different—different ages, different careers, in different places in our lives. We probably wouldn't have been friends outside of this experience, but we shared a common thread in our lives. A desire to get away, to seek adventure, to feed our souls. It wasn't just the actual riding that did that. It was the tiny moments that connected us. When Adrian, the smallest guy on the trip, threw the only ax that stuck in the tree. When one dirt bike flew over the cliff and we used Andy's slack line to pull it back up. James's horrible jokes. Every time we turned back to help when someone ate shit or flipped over his handlebars, then regaled us with commentary on the replay. Moments of vulnerability as we shared our stories around a crackling fire. We were the Breakfast Club in the woods.

It was a new experience that was uncomfortable and challenging. But feeding your soul isn't always about doing things that feel good. It's about doing what makes you feel alive, and alive sometimes lives near death. Darren shredded his shoulder. Greyson twisted his ankle. Sam broke a toe. Everyone went down at one point or another—many times for most of us. We rode on the edge of cliffs where one turn or swerve would have sent us flying into an ocean of rocks hundreds of feet below. But that was the point. Riding the line of fear and flow and finding life in that, something we rarely did at home. The by-product was an honest connection with fellow strangers having a shared experience. And of course for me, shitting in the woods for the very first time. That made me feel alive as fuck. Everything about the experience nourished a part of me I'd always neglected. My soul.

Listen, you don't have to go on motorcycle trips or shit in the woods to feed your soul. You can feed your soul by turning your phone off and reading a good book. Going on a hike. Eating pancakes at your favorite diner and listening to a podcast. Taking yourself to a movie on a Wednesday. Blogging. Telling the guy you're hooking up with how to go down on you, something you've never done in any of your relationships. It's not about the activity. It's about doing something that puts you in touch with the universe. Feeding your soul may mean finally quitting that nine-to-five that's been draining your life for the last ten years and starting a new career, one you're actually passionate about. Or it might mean allowing yourself to eat a few doughnuts without shame or judgment.

Feeding your soul is the action part of building a better relationship with yourself. Giving yourself what you need. Because that's where your truth lives. In your soul. Not in your mind.

You connect to yourself by having a better relationship with your soul.

Get Off the Island or You'll Always Be Tom Hanks Talking to a Volleyball

This last part of Act I is about connecting with others to connect more to yourself. I've put it at the end because you have to do the inner work before you can do the outer work. But don't forget about this piece. Friendships are an important part of building a strong sense of self and confidence. Many believe that gaining confidence is a solitary journey, but it's not. Friends contribute significantly. They can make you believe you can do anything you put your mind to or that you're a piece of shit. You know this because you've had both types of friends throughout your life.

Maybe you've lost your friends after getting into a relationship. So many of us overvalue romantic relationships while undervaluing friendships, which can be just as fulfilling and life-sweetening (and way less traumatic). Perhaps you've found yourself alone and realized that no one asks you to hang out anymore. Or that your last two hundred text messages were all directed to your partner. It's time to break your patterns, to invest in the people who make you laugh, champion your story, and, most important, believe in you.

Flashback: John's Apartment Complex, Dusk, 2005-ish

John drags into his apartment building carrying only his laptop and a Starbucks coffee cup that has seen better days. He makes it halfway up the stairs, then stops. Takes a deep breath, as if he needs to shift his attitude. He straightens a bit. Then continues to the front door.

John enters and instantly stops in his tracks.

EVERYONE (*voice-over*)
Surprise!!!

The apartment is packed like sardines with friends. There must be over thirty people in the tiny one-bedroom. John's wife is standing front and center with a homemade birthday cake.

A long uncomfortable beat. John is frozen and expressionless.

Then suddenly he tosses his stuff on the couch and busts out into windmills. He's break-dancing in the living room, hairs away from hitting his head on furniture.

It's a little weird.

People are confused.

They don't know how to react.
The energy is strange.

FREEZE-FRAME ON JOHN

John is caught mid-windmill, face strained, holding his crotch, his legs spread-eagle.

JOHN (*voice-over*)

This was the first time anyone had thrown me a surprise party. I didn't know what to do. So I just started break-dancing. I think deep inside I felt like I needed to give them something for coming. My first instinct was to make myself a dancing monkey. But it didn't go well.

PAN ACROSS THE UNCOMFORTABLE FACES IN THE ROOM

A few are looking at each other, wondering, What the hell is he doing?

JOHN (*voice-over*)

It was very different than when I did it at my wedding. There was actually a dance floor that time.

FLASH A PHOTO

John is doing windmills in a tuxedo (the same break-dancing move, the only one he still knows how to do) at a lovely bed-and-breakfast on a beautiful farm surrounded by cornfields. Everyone is clapping and smiling. They're impressed. They love it.

BACK TO SCENE—JOHN (*voice-over*)

This was the first time my dancing came from a false place. I used it to deflect, not to connect to myself.

A beat.

JOHN (*voice-over*)

And this was also the first time I realized I had zero friends.

LATER THAT NIGHT

Everyone is now socializing and eating cake. Everyone save John, who is sitting on the counter in the kitchen watching everyone with a half-smile.

JOHN (*voice-over*)

They were all her friends.

FADE OUT

That was the moment I realized I needed my own friends. Yes, all those people were friendly to me. But they were not my friends. I can tell you that because none of them are in my life today. They were my wife's friends and knew me through her. They were not people I had built my own relationships with. My life revolved around someone else, in this case my future ex-wife.

This is common in relationships. When we find someone we want to spend all our time with, we do. And we slowly lose our friends. Not having friends makes us disconnect from ourselves. And when we disconnect from ourselves, we also disconnect from our partner. We think we've found paradise, but we've created our own desert island. Yes, your partner can be your best friend. But he or she cannot be your *only* friend.

I had been disconnecting from myself for so long that I'd become a castaway. I was Tom Hanks talking to a volleyball. It's no wonder I was so unhappy. I didn't think friends were important. I wanted to put all my time and energy into my career because "success" would make me happy. It wasn't until after my divorce that I finally started to put effort into making my own friends. First Sam, then others. And for the first time in my life, the friendships I built were real. Because I was connecting to *me* while connecting to others. Allowing people to see the real John Kim. Not the approval-seeking, insecure John Kim who spun on his head for the wrong reasons.

Dance for you and other people will dance with you. Dance for others and you become a show. Not a person.

We *need* friends. They are not an extra, a luxury, a privilege. Or something we should invest in when we have more time. We are hardwired for human connection. It's ingrained in our biology. When you're hungry, your body is telling you that you need food. When you're crying, your body is telling you that you're hurting and grieving and need to release. When you're tired, your body is telling you that you need sleep. When you're feeling lonely or shitty about yourself, your body is telling you that you need human connection. We forget that human connection comes in many forms besides romance.

I found human connection through a fitness community and through riding motorcycles, smashing burgers, and sharing my story with a group of dudes. I don't know what it will look like for you. But if you don't take action, if you don't put yourself out there, if you don't get out of your house and your head but just keep digging a moat around your castle, you will be depriving yourself of one of your fundamental needs.

Our need to connect is as fundamental as our need for food and water.

—MATTHEW LIEBERMAN

We are tribal creatures. We're not meant to do life alone. And if our social network isn't wide enough, we're going to put too much pressure on the relationships we do have. The person you choose to love isn't your tribe. Your kids are not your tribe. They are a part of your tribe, but not your entire tribe. We get things from our friends that we don't from our partner or our family. Friends are crucial to our growth, journey, and happiness. If you form honest connections with friends, they will help you connect to yourself as well as build your confidence. So you don't have to do it alone.

Do I have a giant collection of friends today who would return my call at three in the morning, bail me out of jail, or help me move (the true test)? I don't know. I haven't called any of my friends at three in the morning to bail me out of jail. I do know that I don't have a giant collection of friends. I have a handful. Some of them I'm closer to than others. And that changes as some relationships grow and some fade. None of them are perfect friends, and I'm not a perfect friend to them. They are real people going through real shit, just like me. Sometimes they're texting while I'm talking. Sometimes they flake. Sometimes they say or do things that hurt or bother me. We don't see eye to eye on life and politics and clothes. But they are my friends. And the friendships are real. They have been built, over time, with trust. We work out together. Ride motorcycles together. Eat together, make fun of each other. The point is, at the end of the day we support each other and champion each other's stories. We truly want the best for each other. Will we be friends forever? Will we grow old together and sit on a porch swing sipping kombucha and reflecting on our lives? I don't know.

No one has perfect friends. As in any relationship, there is no such thing as a perfect friendship. The point is to have real friends. Friends who feel honest to you with where you're at in your life. Friends who encourage your connection to self.

That's how you know if they are real friends.

Your friends may offer resistance or opinions on your choices, but if they don't support your truth and who you truly are becoming, they are not encouraging your connection to yourself. Instead, they are trying to change you. Or they are holding on to the old friendship dynamic between the two of you. Maybe one that worked for you before you started your growth journey. But now the new you makes them uncomfortable. This happens a lot. It's what people mean when they say they are "outgrowing" their friends. It's normal. It's life. **Just because you have a history doesn't mean you have a healthy friendship.** Read that sentence again. As long as you're surrounding yourself with people who hold space for you to be your true self, you'll never be stuck on an island or awkwardly dancing in front of fake friends.

When you're single, it's more important to have good friends than to find a partner.

How to Make Friends
as an Adult

The older we get, the harder it is to make friends. One major reason is the disappearance of plug-and-play social structures after we leave school. When we were younger, friends were delivered to us. They came in the form of field trips, sports teams, social clubs, detention, fraternities, sororities, school dances, and parties. We were one courageous extraverted decision away from entering any one of the micro communities available to us.

Now, as adults, the automatic delivery has stopped. There are no more Postmates for friends. Our communities have shrunk. We have work, the biggest slice of our life pie, the place where we spend most of our time. But many of us don't want to shit where we eat, so we keep our work friends at a distance. Or we've tried to be friends with co-workers and it got weird. Then we have what I call our "residue" friends, the friends from our past. High school or college buddies, friends you've made through your exes, co-workers from previous jobs. But these friends are peripheral. Either you've outgrown them or they were only close friends during a previous period of your life. They are technically friends but not people you do daily life with today. You don't Facetime them while watching an entire episode of *Game of Thrones*.

Some of us have made new friends from hobbies and passions. But the truth is, most of us don't have hobbies or passions. We just work and spend time in our relationship. At this point, if you're married and have children, the friend road forks. Your friend community shrinks even more. You have less time for friends because your priorities have shifted. Seeing a friend becomes an event that has to be planned and scheduled. Like sex these days. You have less in common with your remaining friends and are often at different stages in life.

Most of all, it feels strange to approach strangers to be friends when you're in your thirties and forties. It's weird. They think you want to have sex with them, or they just think there's something wrong with you. You smell desperate. It's not like when we were kids and all it took to make a friend was showing someone what we found in our nose.

With fewer spaces and opportunities to find friends as adults, we have to put more effort into finding and investing in friendships. As adults, we also have more responsibilities and less free time, so finding and investing in friendships usually takes a backseat to all the adulting we're trying to do. Suddenly we have no friends. Now all our happy chips are on our relationship, our children, our family. This of course puts more pressure on our relationship, our children, and our family to make us happy. And that's not fair to them.

Having friends doesn't have to be this hard. It's never too late to build your tribe—in fact, now is the perfect time to do it.

TIME TO MAKE SHIT HAPPEN

1: Set the Intention

Nothing gets done without setting an intention to do it. Friends aren't just going to fall from the sky. You have to set the intention. Tell yourself you want new friends. Put the energy out there. Make the announcement to yourself. Soak it into your subconscious. You'll find yourself making an effort and being more open naturally, without even knowing it.

Making friends isn't usually at the top of our to-do list. It's not on any list really. It's a passing thought we have as we're purposely taking the long way home. Or a matter we usually just let the universe handle. But you can take control of it, and the first step is setting the intention. It's a great muscle to exercise for anything you want in your life.

2: Participate in Communities

Kill two birds with one stone. Pick a passion or interest. Then engage with a community engaged in it. The obvious choice is fitness. If you didn't get the memo, fitness is now done through communities. No one goes to the gym by herself and walks on a treadmill reading *US Weekly* anymore. They do CrossFit, yoga, Pilates, spin, boot camp, boxing. The ways we can find to sweat are endless today, and more spring up all the time.

Get a class pass at the gym and try everything, twice. Congratulations, that's one bird. You're getting something done. The second bird is to engage. Speak to others working out. Socialize with the staff. Put yourself out there. Introduce yourself. Make a joke. Exercise that muscle you haven't used since eighth-grade summer camp.

If exercise isn't your thing, here's something even easier—put down your phone. We are becoming isolated robots by hiding behind our phones. Put down your phone and take advantage of the opportunity to be human again. Focus on what makes us human, like eye contact and smiles. Compliment someone, then get their social media username (the new phone number) and DM them. Follow their feed, like their posts, but also engage with them in person. That's the important piece. Actually speak to them. (I can't believe I'm saying this. But it's the world we live in now.) Phones and social media are just tools. But you can use them to till the soil of friendship. Engaging in person is what makes a relationship real. Otherwise you'll only be pen pals. (If you don't know what a pen pal is, Google it.)

I've used Airbnb's "experiences" to participate in local affordable experiences in my city with a small group. I've gone on two-week Wilderness Collective dirt bike trips with a group of twelve or so. I've also held monthly "9" dinners with a friend: we invite nine strangers to get together and talk about things strangers would never have conversations about. Finally, I've run my own retreats and gatherings. This is how we create our tribes today.

Here are a few more examples of communities to engage with:

Art

Photography

Cooking classes

Writing workshops

Wellness or adventure retreats

Hiking clubs

Rock-climbing groups

Music events

Wellness festivals

Co-working spaces (more important, the events they run)

Fitness events like the Spartan Race or Tough Mudder (if you do it with a small group, the journey naturally produces friendship glue)

3: Don't Say No to Anything Social

Get. The. Fuck. Out. There. Engage with the world. You're not going to make friends by ordering in and watching Netflix every weekend. Stop being so picky about what you like to do and don't like to do. Sometimes the best times happen when we least expect them. Sometimes we meet the coolest people doing the dumbest shit. Get out there and stretch yourself. Doing things that may be uncomfortable is a form of connecting to yourself. You are exploring. Without exploration, there is no connection to self.

So break out of your rut today. Turn your mental dial to "Explore" and lock it there. Accept every invitation. Not necessarily forever. Do it for a couple of days or weeks. See what experiences you have. Either way, you will have stories.

The Annual Friendship Review

This is just between you and me. You're not announcing this to your friends.

Take a long minute and think about all the friends in your life right now.

Then ask yourself these questions. Is each of your friends creating a space for you to connect to yourself? Or are any of them, subtly or not so subtly, pulling you away from yourself? Are they promoting or stunting your growth? How do they treat you? How do they speak to you? Do they want the best for you, or are they always competing with you? Are any of your friendships lopsided? If so, in what way? Are you friends just because of shared history but really have nothing in common anymore? Or do you share the same passions and values? Do your friends give you as much as you give them? Be really honest with yourself here. We make excuses for our friends, especially if they have been in our lives for a long time. No one's hearing how you answer this question. So it's okay. Be real. Be honest.

Maybe you have a friend who doesn't support who you really are or champion your story. Or maybe this friend is just draining and negative, always making everything about them. Have you made an effort to address the issue? Have you given them an opportunity to change? If so, and they have done nothing to step it up, **it's time to start investing less in this friendship and more in other ones.** An announcement is not necessary. Breaking up with friends is different from breaking up with a partner. There is no breakup. There is only a fading-out. All you have to do is allow people to go their own way, naturally. You start.

And in case you need to hear it again:

1. Set the intention to make new friends.

2. Pick a community you want to engage with.

3. Put yourself out there and say yes to everything.

Relationship Residue

(Letting Go)

There are far, far better things ahead than
any we have left behind.

—C. S. LEWIS

Like I said in the beginning, this is not a book about how to have a better relationship. This is a book about how to have a better relationship with yourself. The irony, though, is that no force has a greater impact on the relationship you have with yourself than the relationships you have had with others.

Our past relationships define us. They lay the tracks. They print the blueprints we follow. But most important, they either connect us to ourselves or disconnect us from ourselves. Simply put, healthy relationships *encourage* us to connect with ourselves. Unhealthy relationships *prevent* us from connecting with ourselves.

But in order to redefine ourselves, we must first look at what happened in our past. In coaching thousands about their relationships, I've discovered a pattern. Although everyone's love story is different, the overarching journey of love that we all go through is pretty much the same.

Our Love Journey in a Shot Glass

Young Love: The Sticky

In high school, our attraction is based on two things.

1. IDENTITY

We find attractive what we lack in ourselves. Yes, on the surface you may think his handsome face and the way his cute butt jiggles when he scrambles to throw the Hail Mary touchdown is "super-hot." But how much of wanting him has to do with others wanting him too and so you think that, if you got him, you'd be worth more? Would your friends think you were cooler if the prom queen was actually your girlfriend and not just spank material in the shower?

Of course, it's not the '50s, and jocks and prom queens aren't the only people we are attracted to in high school anymore. We also love the guy in the band, the cool nerd, the skater, and so on. My point is, these are not people we're noticing. They are identities. In high school, we are all just putty being formed. We have no inner shape. We define and find our worth in others. So it makes sense that love starts for us at this age with what someone looks like to us—not necessarily their heart or character.

2. WHAT SMELLS FAMILIAR

Chaos. Impulsiveness. Unpredictability. Reactiveness. Control. Neediness. Codependency. Enmeshment. Basically the relationship dynamic we grew up with at home. Whatever it is, we believe this is what love looks like because it's all we know. When it comes to love, we have not taken our Hero's Journey. We don't yet know any different. Healthy is foreign to many of us. Boring even.

If we believe we are lacking and need to find value and identity in someone else, we are powerless in the relationship. If we chase only what smells familiar, because no one's family is perfect and no child enters adulthood unscarred, we are re-creating trauma, not building love.

When we combine finding our value in someone else with what smells familiar, we get unhealthy dysfunctional love that feels fucking amazing.

I call it "the sticky."

The sticky is made up of warped definitions of love, pursued down a bumpy road of chaos and reactivity. Unhealthy conflict. Internalization. Doing things you probably wouldn't normally do. Sacrificing voice, compromising self, and puncturing self-esteem instead of growing it. Did I mention the sticky feels amazing? That's because drama, jealousy, control, and chasing get intense and it's easy to mistake intensity for love.

It's not your fault—that's all you know and have experienced.

Young love is instinctual. The rush of skinny-dipping. You don't think about what happens when you have to get out of the water.

Our Twenties: Losing Yourself in Someone Else

Most of our twenties is about splattering paint, blindfolded, and hoping to see a beautiful painting when we're done. We try to make a beeline down a well-lighted path toward a secure future. But that's impossible. We don't know what we want yet. And we haven't experienced enough to give us the maps to even find that path. Like picking a major in college, what we want will change a thousand times. Life is undeclared. But we don't know that in our twenties. We believe we're on our way.

The truth is, there is no path in our twenties. There is a big field of thorns and booby traps. But there are also lakes and waterfalls to do backflips off of. Most of us have not turned the corner and become curious about ourselves and why we do what we do. We are still walking reactions bouncing off our experiences like pinballs. We wear adult clothes and go out to fancy dinners we can't afford.

Since we're still finding ourselves, we go by what we feel. Not what we believe is healthy for us. Typically, our choices lead to a lot of pain.

Enter empty sex. One-night stands. Experimentation. Lots of people-pleasing, especially in the bedroom. Sketchy situations where you should have ended up in a trunk. Zero self-care. A life diet based on validation and approval. Not expressing yourself, speaking up, and asking for what you want. Staying in relationships for way too long. Or not long enough.

Most people end up in their first serious relationship around this time, and so it begins: Ordering in. Binge-watching. Losing friends as you lose yourself in your person. And eventually, emotional claustrophobia as you naturally grow and want to become your own person. Enter jealousy and control and rage from your confused partner, who is not ready and doesn't understand why you don't "love" them anymore.

This decade is like a car crash. And many people in their twenties will make a few more laps around that crazy track before it's over.

If you're reading this book, you're probably done with all that. No more runs on the crazy train. You want something different, and you're sick of people judging you because you're young. You're willing to look inward. You want to break old patterns and gain the self-awareness to live life thoughtfully and with a strong sense of inner strength. Well, you can. Because self-betterment doesn't discriminate by age. It discriminates by intention. If your heart's in the right place and you're willing to do the work, this book can be the first domino that starts your journey.

Our Thirties and Forties: Starting the Search for the True Self

If our twenties is a car crash, our thirties and forties are a car wash.

We're done with the old. Done with codependency and enmeshment. Done with walking on eggshells and faking orgasms, with screaming matches and noncommunication. Done taking care of people. Done not being heard.

We are thirsty for something new. We are finally interested in ourselves. In who we are and where we want to go. And how we want to be treated.

Our thirties is when all the anger and resentment we've buried for so long raises its ugly head. When that happens, everyone feels it. Your partner. Your friends. Your family. Your boss and your co-workers. Things that were important to you don't matter as much now. The old you collapses like the marionette after the puppet master lets go of the strings. And new things start to matter. New things you hang your happiness on.

Lines are now drawn. Boundaries are formed. Some friends fade. Some stay. This is when a lot of us find yoga, or get sober, or start meditating.

If you've been in a relationship since your early twenties, this is also when that "seven-year itch" appears. When people start to outgrow each other. When one or both parties want something different. When comfort is no longer enough. Some may be emotionally in the same place and will make it through the turbulence and change together. They'll jump out of the plane together before it goes down. But to be honest, most relationships don't end that way.

And that's okay. If you've only been with one person for most of your life, you're going to be curious. There's nothing wrong with you for being curious, and maybe there's nothing wrong with the relationship either. Curiosity just means you're human. It's normal to be curious and attracted to other people, especially if you haven't experienced other people. And it's not just about sex. You're curious about a different dynamic. You've had the same meal for years, while your taste buds were still forming. Being curious doesn't mean you should break up or cheat. It's a real thing, though, and should be explored, not buried. Whatever you push down will always come back up.

Growth can't happen without new experiences. Love is no exception. The good news is that you can have these new experiences with the same person. But only if both of you put effort into growing, changing, and evolving together by growing, changing, and evolving individually. **You have to grow individually if you want to grow as a couple.** If not, two become one and you're back in your twenties. Your thirties is when you need to take ownership and work through your shit.

The car wash of our thirties and forties is about finally growing up. By going on a journey of finding and connecting to yourself.

Of course, not everyone's love journey is the same. I'm painting here with broad strokes, based on common themes from my clients' stories. But maybe you can relate to some if not all of it. Now is the time to ask yourself one of the most important questions you'll ever ask yourself.

How do I create healthy new love experiences that will eclipse the old ones—and pave over the unhealthy ones—and give me new definitions of love?

Even if you are in a relationship now, this is the time to ask this question. Because relationships are not a constant. They are always changing, evolving, and growing, and your relationship with yourself is always changing, evolving, and growing as well. You don't have to be in a new love experience to give yourself a new love experience. You can make the one you're in now a new love experience.

Boots and Boners

Maddy met Dave at a country music festival called Stagecoach. They tell people that Garth Brooks was their Cupid, since he was the artist playing onstage when their eyes locked across the crowd. Everything happened very fast from there. A few wild nights of Jack Daniels, country love songs, and passion and suddenly they were living together and arguing about how the dishes should be put away.

Although their sexual attraction was off the charts, Maddy and Dave spoke very different love languages and had very different definitions of love. Maddy's love language was touch and words of affirmation. Dave's was "just sex." That's not technically a love language, but he believed it was. He defined love based on how much sex they had. If they weren't having sex, he felt unloved and rejected. If they were having a lot of sex, he felt loved and desired. But Maddy didn't enjoy sex. She usually just did it for him. This made Dave feel tricked, because she had presented herself as "a highly sexual person" when they first met but after a year he realized she wasn't. They came to me as a last resort.

"All Dave cares about are his boots and boners," Maggie sighed. As we started processing, though, I realized this wasn't about sex. It was about distorted definitions of love. Dave had always equated love with sex. That idea had started early on with pornographic images, which wired him a certain way. It was reinforced by "guy talk" in locker rooms (he played sports in high school and college) and through relationships with women who also defined love as sex. It was all he knew. But as it turned out, most of those women had been sexually abused in ways that disconnected them from their bodies and wired them to be highly sexual. It came out that Maddy was also sexually abused, which Dave didn't know. But she had gone the other way in reaction to that trauma. She didn't enjoy sex. Sex was a device, something she used to attract men. Not something that brought her pleasure.

Once I knew this, I knew their focus needed to be giving themselves new love experiences to create new definitions of love and lay new tracks. I knew that as they started the journey of creating new definitions of love, each of them would naturally be forced to look inward and explore their past traumas.

Maddy's individual work was to process her abuse and start a new relationship with her body and sex. Dave's individual work was to explore why he connected love and desire only with sex and sexual acts and not with all the nonsexual ways we can show love and desire. Dave realized that he had never experienced true intimacy, and neither had Maddy. Once they both realized this, they were suddenly on the same team and thirsty for a new love experience.

They began to explore sex and intimacy in a new way and actually communicated in the bedroom for the first time in their lives. Understanding each other better was crucial. They learned to ask for their needs to be met, but they also respected each other's needs. As Maddy worked through her trauma and explored her own sexuality and dropped into her body, she became more comfortable and adventurous in the bedroom. It was no longer just about pleasing men. Now she wanted to please herself. It turns out she *was* sexual. Her sexuality was just suppressed. Dave learned to be intimate through kissing and words and slow touch and eye contact, everything his locker-room buddies called "gay." They created a new love experience together, and by doing so, they created a new definition of sex and intimacy and laid new tracks for their relationship. These changes rippled outward. They felt closer and more connected as a couple. With their new connection, Dave and Maddy both felt like their sex life became more intimate and satisfying. Theirs was a new type of sex that wasn't just about skin and orgasms but about exploration and a deeper love.

Clearing out your relationship residue can bring self-awareness you never had before. I know I can relate to Dave's story. I also used to tightly connect love to sex. Feeling loved and desired was based on how much sex I was getting. Which meant I put a lot of pressure on my girlfriends to have sex with me even if they didn't feel like it. It wasn't until I started to give myself a new love experience as well as work through my own shit that I created new definitions of sex and intimacy.

Reiki Hands

You will meet her later, so I don't want to give away her name just yet. But she was someone I met on a blind date. I didn't kiss her until our second date, and we didn't have sex until weeks later, which made her question if I was even into her. I usually pursue hard and fast, but this time was different. She caught me at a time in my life when I was thirsty for something deeper. And I didn't know what that looked or felt like because I'd always chased skin first. This time I wanted sex to be the by-product, not the buy-in.

My new love experience didn't come in a deep, meaningful, life-changing conversation about what sex and intimacy can look like. It came in a single touch. A moment. It wasn't how she touched me. It wasn't about technique. It was the energy, intention, and curiosity behind her touch. I know that sounds hokey and abstract, but let me explain. All I knew was the two-dimensional feeling of feeling good, especially this early into getting to know someone. The sugar, the dopamine, the gift of someone wanting to pleasure you. The skin-deep feelings, not the underlying energy, loaded with intention. And that's what I felt this time. Like energy work, her touch pierced deeper and gave me more than pleasure. It gave me patience. There was a story there. A spirit. An openness and vulnerability. I felt it. And that's when I thought to myself, *There is something different here.*

This was the beginning of wanting something new.

The Search for Love Starts Earlier than You Think

I remember watching the movie *Weird Science* when I was twelve. If you don't know, it's about two nerdy teens who create their perfect woman, "Lisa," after hooking up wires to a Barbie doll and wearing bras on their heads. The '80s were a weird time with weird movies. Anyway, the doll comes to life and teaches them about love and life. The first time I remember desiring a woman was while I was watching this movie.

I literally sat in my parents' room (where I watched movies), mouth open, eyes shut tight, wishing for some weird science to happen to me. I really wanted a woman to pull me out of my boring world and show me a new one. But Kelly LeBrock never walked in. Only my mom, to ask me if I was hungry.

It wasn't just the lips and curves and the growing curiosity of a twelve-year-old. It was also the idea of having a new type of friend. One who made you feel something different. One who would take care of you. One who understood you.

This was the first time it was imprinted on my subconscious that finding someone else (a woman) would bring me happiness. With that person, I would be valuable, accepted. Other twelve-year-old dudes would be jealous of me. It was the beginning of a long journey of not wanting to be alone. I would spend the next thirty years of my life looking for my "Lisa."

For you, it probably didn't start with an '80s movie about a doll coming to life as a supermodel. But it started somewhere. Maybe it was watching the lovers Romeo and Juliet dying for each other, or all the Disney princess movies with a woman being saved by a man and living happily ever after. Or witnessing a soaked Ryan Gosling confessing his undying love in *The Notebook*. Or your parents telling you over and over that you needed to find someone so you could start a family and be happy. And of course, today we get the added pressure of social media. Engagements. Weddings. Exotic honeymoons. Photos of couples traveling the world and feeding each other pizza. Kids on swings. Perfect little families. We all know these photos show life through a giant filter that hides the splinters in the white picket fence. Relationships take a shit ton of work, and no relationship is flawless. But we still buy into the illusion and believe that we are less than because our lives don't look like the images that surround us.

All of this drives us to search for love, for "the one." We approach this search like our life depends on it. It becomes our Holy Grail. But we never learn about the smaller steps in the process, the dynamics of a real relationship and how to have a healthy one. We don't learn about codependency, attachment styles, and healthy boundaries, or about why we behave the way we do in love. We are just thrown into the forest to stumble around and learn what we can from our fall(s). With no tools or knowledge of what a healthy relationship actually looks like, we love strictly with what we feel and what we're used to. Love then becomes a knee-jerk response to the other person stemming from our wounds, a way to fill holes in ourselves.

Your idea of love may be based on what you saw in your parents' behavior, which, for many of you, was dysfunctional and unhealthy. If so, you have probably fallen into unhealthy relationships marked by codependency, jealousy, control, and even physical and emotional abuse. Maybe you always began to lose yourself in these relationships, but stayed in them. You had come to believe that this was what loving someone looked like—sacrifice. Until you woke up one day and didn't know *either* of the people in the mirror. You had been completely oblivious to how you actually felt just because you were too afraid to be alone, and so was your partner brushing his teeth behind you.

Coming up, I want to give you some of the tools that a lot of you missed out on so that you can define healthy, both for yourself and for what that looks like with other people. It starts with clearing away the cobwebs.

Tracy Chapman
Saved My Life

I was sitting in my car because I had nowhere else to go. It was rainy and dark, and just minutes after my wife found porn on my computer. She grew up conservative. Me watching porn was like me cheating on her. I kept playing back the disappointment and hurt etched on her face as I sat there thinking about my life.

Porn was a regular thing for me during that time. It was my way of coping with the fact that nothing good was going on in my life. My marriage was falling apart. My writing career was going nowhere. Watching porn was the only way to numb myself. But that was no excuse. I had lied to my wife. I had told her I didn't watch that stuff when I did.

As the rain fell, I wondered for the first time if I had a problem. My dad was an alcoholic, so I knew addiction was in my blood. It was the lowest point in my life. I felt so alone and useless. Then, while I just sat there in my car, staring blankly out at nothing, Tracy Chapman began playing on the radio. "If you knew that you would die today. If you saw the face of God and love, would you change?" It felt as though she was speaking directly to me. Like she was following my story and wrote that song for the universe to present to me at that exact moment. I sat there reviewing my life and how unhappy I was. Then the rain abruptly stopped, as if the sky wanted me to answer her question. One shaky word emerged from a rumble of fear and pain.

Yes.

Suddenly I was going to SAA (Sex Addicts Anonymous) and SLAA (Sex and Love Addicts Anonymous) meetings. I started to see a therapist. Again. I started reading self-help and relationship books. I started to learn about me. I learned that my views of love were distorted and unhealthy. I thought that love meant, if I go down, you go down with me. And vice versa. I thought love meant we become one person.

I remember one incident in my marriage. After a long day of working on the set, she wanted to hang out with her co-star in his hotel room. It was an after-party and there would be others there as well. It wouldn't be just them. But I remember not approving of this and telling her, "It's not what married people do." I remember ruining a special night for her—the closing of a big film project—by overreacting and using marriage to hide behind my codependency and insecurity. That was one of many times I was controlling because I didn't have a sense of self.

My definitions of love and how to be loving came from blueprints I had carried with me my entire life. They were sketched out by my parents and their culture, then inked in by my fears and patterns from other love experiences. And of course, they were reinforced by messages I got from the larger world. I also didn't have any tools. I didn't practice self-awareness or take ownership. I couldn't see the world through anything but my own tainted lenses. I was defensive and reactive. I grabbed instead of held. I didn't know that relationships meant constantly looking inward, expressing your truth, and holding a safe space for your partner. It wasn't until a decade later—after years of therapy and many more expired relationships—that I acquired the tools to actually execute this.

My first memory of looking inward and holding a safe space was when my girlfriend at the time came home and expressed that I hadn't been very present lately. I remember instantly feeling defensive. I was going through a stressful time and also paying all the bills, including hers. But instead of trying to be understood, I tried to understand. She was right. I was constantly in deep thought or on my phone when we were together. I apologized without defending myself like I usually did. I realized that defensiveness would not create a space safe enough for her to express her needs. That she would respond by suppressing her feelings. That we would start to drift.

I used to think love just meant you like someone because you think they're hot and everything works out because you guys love each other so much and that's all that matters. Love will conquer all, right? But that's not love. That's a fairy tale I bought into many many years ago. Taking ownership and creating a space is what it means to love. Looking inward without defensiveness is what it means to love. And giant fights are not the only time to do that. Love happens in the daily mundane, like when my girlfriend told me I didn't seem present. She didn't have a huge problem with me. She just wanted me to be more present. It was a simple ask that the old me would have turned into an emotional argument that left her feeling unsafe. I realized I had grown.

That moment sitting in my car with Tracy Chapman was the beginning of the end. The beginning of the new me. The end of my marriage. As I started to go to meetings and take a really good honest look at myself, for the first time in my life, I decided I wasn't happy writing screenplays anymore. I was doing it for the wrong reasons. Just going through the motions. It didn't give me a sense of purpose. So I went back to grad school to study psychology and become a therapist. I thought if I couldn't move people by the masses, I would do it one at a time. Meanwhile, my wife was gaining traction in her career. She was booking projects left and right and traveling often. The busier we got, the more we drifted. Then one day, via Skype, she asked for a separation, which quickly turned into a divorce.

Many of you reading this might be going through a breakup, or what I call an "expired relationship." Or you're in a relationship now but struggle with being fully present because you haven't moved on from your previous one. Or the one before that. Maybe you told yourself you have but you know deep down you haven't because old unresolved issues are impacting your current relationship. You know you need to do something about it but don't really know where to start. Either way, expired relationships are something we all go through.

Most of us don't know how to maneuver through an expired relationship. The bad news is that there is no blanket formula. It's different for everyone, depending on your story and the impact the relationship had on you. But maybe by sharing what I went through, as well as some of my clients, I can help you see something you hadn't seen before, or help you reframe what happened, or spark something in you that sets you off on your journey. Because you can't build anything healthy and sustainable with someone else until you've let go of the old.

What Moving On Really Looks Like

'm not a big fan of the term "moving on." I mean, if it's been four years, it may be time to move forward with your life. But usually we slam ourselves with the need to "move on" only a few weeks after the breakup. The trouble is, pushing yourself to move on discredits the depth of what happened and also hands you a ticking clock, which adds even more pressure to move on. Everything that has happened in that relationship, good or bad, is a part of your story and a part of you. If you reject parts of your story, you are rejecting and thus disconnecting with parts of yourself. I understand that your relationship may have been toxic and abusive. But you don't heal by rejecting it, ripping it out, and not looking at it. You're actually keeping those flames going. The anger and hurt will continue to glow. If you really want to move on, start with acceptance.

Acceptance is the beginning of any healing. When we don't accept something, it continues to grow, like a virus. We may be able to bury it for a while by distracting ourselves, but it will eventually come back. By rejecting it, denying it, pretending like it never happened, or minimizing its ongoing impact on us, we actually continue to feed it, allowing it to grow until it makes us destructive—to ourselves, to other people, or to another relationship. Whether you're dealing with a job loss, an illness, or an expired relationship, acceptance is the first and the most important step to getting past it.

Acceptance doesn't mean you want to get back together with your ex. If you do in fact want to get back together with your ex, then you must accept that as your truth and start there. Maybe you need to accept how much you've been hurt so you can start grieving the loss of the relationship. Maybe you need to accept that it wasn't your fault. Or that it was—maybe you need to take ownership so you'll be better in your next relationship. Maybe acceptance means forgiveness. Maybe acceptance means boundaries. Ask yourself what you need to start accepting and what that looks like for you. And remember, acceptance is a process. It takes time. It's not something you do over a weekend. What's important is that you start the process.

As you start to accept what happened, you will naturally start to move on. I'm going to give you another new definition: **You are not moving on. You are moving through.** Acceptance isn't a corner you turn. It's a journey, and journeys take time. But eventually a journey can lead you back to the village a changed person, because with every journey there is a transformation. You have to go through the process. You are grieving. You are sad. You are angry, and you are allowing yourself to be angry. You have looked at the crash and taken ownership for your part. You have examined the black box. Learn the lessons and apply them to your life. You are a better version of yourself because of what happened and everything you learned from it about love, life, and, most important, yourself.

Acceptance allows you to start moving through, past what happened, so you're finally able to let go and be present in what you're in now. With acceptance, you can finally pull your other foot out of the sticky past and plant both feet in the present—the relationship you're building with yourself, and then with someone else. Let's explore what moving through looks like in action.

"My Pus*y Knows Things"

J essica had a large Instagram following. She lifted weights, rode motorcycles, and documented a lot of badassery. This meant "moving on" was only a few DMs away. She was going through her sixth expired relationship when she contacted me. Jessica usually got over someone in about three months. And then under someone else in about the same amount of time. But this time was different. It had been seven months, and she couldn't manage to "get over" her ex and had no desire to be with anyone else. "It's like my pussy died. Or it's trying to protect me or tell me something. Maybe it knows things."

She must have felt awkward as I just stared back, expressionless at her joke. But I actually felt she was on to something. Not necessarily about her vagina, but about her body. The fact that she "couldn't get it up" meant something. I believe it was her body trying to tell her something, something that she was trying not to hear. Or maybe she wasn't in a place to hear it. Until now.

As we worked through this together, I learned that Jessica grew up with a single mom and a false belief that men always leave. Dad was in the picture for a split second before he split. She'd had no communication with him since. Her early imprints of love were boyfriends who either cheated or left. As she grew up, she started to lose herself in men. She would do anything to keep them from leaving. This meant repressing her feelings, ignoring red flags, and always putting their needs before her own. And of course, most of them did leave. This hardened her heart and cemented her false belief. By the time she was in her late twenties, her relationships were lasting only about six months and her partners weren't the ones leaving. She was.

Like a stripper uses the stage to get her power back, Jessica used Instagram as a way to feel wanted and desired on her terms. The more she grew her following, the more suitors she had. She would date many of them, then leave them before they left her. I asked her if she had ever been in love, and she admitted that she had. Twice. Before she was "Instafamous." As we processed both relationships, I realized that this was the first time she had actually talked about them and acknowledged them as losses. She had never grieved those relationships. Instead, she flipped a switch and decided to "move on." We spent many of the following sessions just focusing on her loss. Accepting what she had once. The joy of each of the people she'd loved. The power of the connection she had with each one. They weren't bad dudes. They were just young, like her.

When a relationship is over, there is loss. So many of us don't see that. Or we don't want to see that because of our pain, fear, and anger. We don't accept the good parts. We don't allow ourselves to miss them, afraid that will mean that the one we lost, or the relationship, still has power over us. But it's not about power. It's about two people who shared their hearts and did the best they could. And a relationship is no less real for being unhealthy. There are real memories there. No matter how bad something was, there were still moments of magic and connection and laughter, and now you've lost that.

If you don't grieve the death of the relationship and allow yourself to feel everything you have lost but instead just push it down, you will cope in other ways. If not with sex, drugs, or food, then maybe by jumping from relationship to relationship. Whatever you haven't grieved is the virus you will carry into all of them.

"My Wife Won't Give
Me Blow Jobs Anymore"

There are some clients you just don't like. They annoy the shit out of you. Sometimes you can't really put your finger on why. Yes, they're defensive, argumentative, and don't want to do the work. But that's not why you don't like them. The problem is not where they're at. It's who they are. They're people you probably wouldn't hang out with in "real life." And they keep coming back, which is what annoys you the most, because as a therapist you can't tell your clients to not come back because they annoy the shit out of you. I mean, you *can*, but you'll probably end up in the back pages of one of those therapist magazines that list all the therapists who have lost their license.

Jon was one of those clients. He didn't come for himself. He was sent. This happens a lot in my world. Usually men are sent to me by their girlfriends and wives, who think they're sending their men to behavior camp, convinced they will magically return with manners, emotional tools, and a newfound appreciation for life and their partner. Jon told me his wife heard me on "Dax's podcast," which he hadn't listened to himself. His wife thought I could give him some "relationship tricks."

So many things about the first words that came out of Jon's mouth had already annoyed me. Why did he have to mention that he didn't listen to my episode on "Dax's podcast"? (By the way, the podcast is called *Armchair Expert*, not "Dax's podcast," like he knows Dax personally or something.) I'll tell you why. Because he wanted me to know that I wasn't better than him. And of course, that he only wanted "relationship tricks" from me. He was too cool for therapy. So he used a phrase that made me sound like a dog trainer. I would have been less annoyed if he'd come in and just said, "Listen, Kimbo, I don't believe in therapy. I don't believe in you. I'm just here because my wife won't give me blow jobs anymore. Fix it." If Jon had said those exact words, I would have fucking loved him. That kind of honesty would have broken down so many walls.

Instead, it would take many sessions to finally discover that he felt that way. Jon had never gone to therapy because he didn't believe in it. He didn't like me because his wife followed me on social media and listened to my podcasts, even bought one of my relationship audio courses (which he made sure to mention he hadn't listened to either). And this whole thing started because she wouldn't give him road head on the way home from Joshua Tree one night. Of course, it wasn't about the head. It was about him not being present in his marriage because he wasn't over his previous relationship.

Let's call her Sally. Sally from the Valley. Jon met Sally when they were in their midtwenties. It was that sticky codependent young love that has you losing yourself in each other. But since Jon had never gone to therapy, he didn't know it wasn't healthy love. He just remembered how intense it was and how much Sally loved going down on him. But did she really? Or was she afraid to lose him? Did she maybe think that's what a good girlfriend does? I never met Sally, but I'm pretty sure she wasn't obsessed with Jon's penis like he claimed she was.

As we continued to process his relationship with Sally, Jon started to realize how much she had hurt him when she broke up with him. He realized he never really grieved that loss. He never accepted or moved through it. Instead, he compared all the other relationships after that to Sally from the Valley because that relationship had made the deepest love imprint on him.

He finally allowed himself to feel all the pain from that expired relationship. As we followed that string down, we discovered more old wounds from growing up with an alcoholic mother who changed men like socks, toxic men who bullied Jon and gave him a warped definition of a man. He realized how unhealthy his relationship with Sally actually was. This made him question if it had really been love. He finally watched the whole documentary instead of just playing the romance movie trailer over and over again. These realizations gave him fresh lenses and a newfound appreciation for his wife and what they were building. With this new perspective, Jon was able to be fully present in his relationship with her and to create a new definition of love, one that wasn't based on others. He was able to build something new. Something fresh. Something healthy. Something real.

Two things about the clients who resist therapy: One, you realize you actually do like them once you see the real person, with a real story, hiding behind that resistance. Two, you realize their initial resistance reminded you of yourself. Jon's story hit home for me, hard. I could relate to what he was going through. I have also compared my relationships with previous ones. I'd judged current loves with older imprints because the feeling of that young love in the past was so powerful. I hadn't yet learned that relationship dysfunction feels like crack cocaine. And that's what I was chasing. Not love. Real love doesn't knock your socks off. Real love holds up a mirror.

My Next Love Experience (Moving Through)

I was finally ready to date again. I was connecting to myself through my work and to my body through CrossFit. I finally had a sense of self, an Asian friend, and a thirst for a new love experience. But other than one sloppy make-out session on the dance floor of a Ktown nightclub and some scattered flirting at a few parties, I didn't find anyone I connected with. Being single sucked.

Meanwhile, I started a blog on Tumblr, back when Tumblr was a thing. I called it *The Angry Therapist*. I thought it was funny that a therapist could be angry. But to be honest, it was more sad than funny. I had been angry for most of my life. And this anger was a giant brick wall that prevented me from really getting to know myself. By blogging and expressing my truth, I slowly started chipping away at this wall. I started to discover myself through this little blog. *The Angry Therapist* became my secret passion. A digital journal just for me. I didn't think anyone would read it.

In between posting, I would scroll through my feed. One

day, a post caught my eye. A pretty American girl in Japan. She posted a WOD (Workout Of the Day): running backwards in her neighborhood. This drew my attention because it was a CrossFit thing. That and the fact that she was a white southern girl who spoke fluent Japanese. I thought that was pretty rad. Okay, and her thick long hair and soft brown eyes. But she was taken, so I didn't have any intentions. Honestly. I was more fascinated by her life in Japan and the culture there. I've always wanted to visit Japan.

So we became "internet friends" and would comment on each other's posts. She wanted advice on her relationship because it was expiring. I didn't see this news as an opportunity. What started as requesting and giving advice turned into months and months of long-winded emails back and forth about life, love, and dreams. Meanwhile, I was still finding myself. Got some tattoos. Bought a motorcycle. She ended up breaking up with her boyfriend and decided to move back home to Georgia. We kept writing long letters to each other like lovers separated by war. Except we weren't lovers. Well, until I finally visited her in Georgia and we kissed on the patio of some random restaurant bar. This turned into a long-distance relationship until she moved to LA six months later.

We dated for the next two and a half years. She was gentle and kind and treated me better than anyone had before. She made me feel like I hung the moon. And I've never felt that way in any relationship. She cooked me shrimp and grits. Held me with two hands. Championed my work. Created a safe space that gave me a sense of worth. She was the first girl who rode on the back of my motorcycle. She did art. I wrote. We were young and free and our love felt like a '60s film.

But then it started to fade. We started to grow apart. Wait, maybe I should use "I" statements, like I encourage my clients to do. It was me. Not her. I was confused. I wasn't there anymore. And I didn't know why. Maybe it was getting too serious and I wasn't ready to settle down. I found myself starting to criticize her and pick her apart. I was sabotaging. Bullying. Or maybe testing to see if she would stick up for herself. I don't know, but I didn't like who I was being. A pouty child who didn't want to finish his meal.

Instead of facing my feelings of disconnect, I allowed myself to drift and blamed it on fading chemistry between us. I checked out. Finally, I decided to end it. It was one of the hardest things I ever had to do. Not only because nothing was technically wrong with our relationship, but because she didn't see it coming. Ending a relationship without warning can be an act of violence. I know this. I've seen the effects of it on my clients. I was suddenly the asshole people go see a therapist for.

It wasn't until a year after I ended the relationship and was in my own therapy that I realized I hadn't just been a dick. I had looked for holes and purposely sabotaged the relationship because I was subconsciously comparing it to my marriage. It was the first relationship I had after my divorce. It didn't feel as intense as my marriage had been, and I mistook lack of intensity for lack of love. Of course it didn't feel as intense. Because it was healthier and I had grown. Or had I?

The thing about growth is that it isn't a constant. Just because you've done work on yourself doesn't mean you're done or won't snap back into old ways. We are like rubber bands. Working on yourself is a never-ending process, not a onetime thing. We connect and disconnect with ourselves constantly, depending on where we're at in our lives, what we're going through, and the quality of our relationships.

People think that when you get into a relationship, the work stops. You're done. You've made it. You've found someone. You've reached the island. Thank God! You don't have to "date yourself" (aka work on yourself) anymore. But the truth is, even more self-work is needed when you're in a relationship than when you're single. Because now the chances of you returning to who you used to be before you embarked on your self-betterment journey are much greater.

Here's why. First, the obvious. You are now sharing with another person all the time you were spending on yourself. That's the whole point, isn't it? You're choosing to share your life with someone. So you should. But as routines and schedules blend, the new priority in your life becomes the relationship instead of what it was before—you. This makes it easy to stop pedaling your connection-to-self bike. It's easy to forget about the alone time you need to recharge, to drop that yoga class you never missed when you were single. Everything is now a compromise. You do what your partner likes. Then you do what you like. His favorite restaurant. Your favorite restaurant. Her favorite type of movie. Then yours. Theoretically, you two like some of the same things or you probably wouldn't be together. This overlap of tastes and likes is the shaded space in the relationship Venn diagram labeled "in common." It can be anything from food to values to life direction. Where the two of you don't share shaded space is called "compromise." It is a healthy and normal fact that all relationships have that space. However, there is a difference between compromise and compromise of self. This is the not so obvious and more important reason why you need to keep pedaling your own bike when you're in a relationship, and why being single on purpose is *not* just for singles.

When you're single, you're just dealing with your own shit—all your triggers, addictions, unhealthy tugs, thought patterns, and behaviors that keep you stunted and stuck at yesterday. When you're in a relationship, you're now dealing with your shit plus someone else's shit too. Since everyone has shit, this is unavoidable. If you have a story, you have shit. How much of it you've worked through depends on how much you've worked on you.

But here's the thing. When you stop working on yourself, you start drifting. First, with yourself. You start compromising your sense of self. You start negotiating again. You fall back into old patterns. You snap back. Your relationship with yourself starts to collapse. You know less about who you are today. You feel confused and unsure of what you want. You don't feel good about yourself. Then, because this changes the dynamic of the relationship, you start drifting away from your partner. Or your partner starts drifting away from you. Or both of you drift away. It is at *this* point that most couples drop the ball. The relationship is directly impacted when they stop pedaling their own bike, stop building their relationship with themselves.

Think about all the times when you thought you were on your path, growing and becoming a better version of yourself, then fell in love and found yourself regressing. It happens to everyone. Even therapists.

Street Art, a Parrot, and Long Hair I Couldn't Pull Off

By now, four years after my divorce, I had built a tribe. I had my motorcycle and barbell friends from CrossFit. I had Sam, Joey, and Ronaldo—my "crepes and cappuccino" friends I could have heartfelt conversations with over coffee and talk about things men don't usually talk about, like how we felt about ourselves. I also had a few female friends, which never happened when I was married. When we were married, my ex-wife had tons of guy friends, and I was always jealous of that. Now it was catch-up time. It felt good to just be friends with women for once, without wanting anything more. But of course, that didn't last long.

One night one of my best female friends took me out for my birthday. I'll call her Patricia. We met at the CrossFit Box and had gotten close because we were both on a path of bettering ourselves. We spoke the same language. She was also divorced and had come to Los Angeles to start over. She had dreams of working as a 3-D artist in Hollywood, but that dream eventually faded and she found her calling and passion in street art, for which she had a natural gift. When we went out for my birthday, we ended up kissing. Or more accurately, I had one beer (that's all it takes) and kissed her, and she kissed me back. Then things happened really fast. They often do when you have a friendship as a foundation. It's like the relationship climbs into the *Millennium Falcon* and you go light speed.

We moved in together. We got a parrot who whistled Dr. Dre's "Next Episode," and I grew my hair long. I'd always wanted to do that but didn't because I couldn't get past the in-between stage. We went grocery-shopping together. Worked out together. Spray-painted street art all over Los Angeles together. Had lots of crazy sex—sex with her was the first time I used sex toys, which opened up a whole new world, one without judgment and shoulds. It was the dream of every boy turned man come true. By making them real, she helped me lift the shame off the pornographic images I'd grown up watching before I was ready. But more important, she made them okay.

It was a powerful relationship. It made me feel like we were two kids ditching school. No one needed to understand us. We just needed to understand us. She was an amazing girlfriend and a beautiful person. We also had both come out of love tunnels, so we had some awareness and tools. Finally! We were adults loving responsibly. We had our own lives. We expressed ourselves. I finally had a sense of self. I was finally connecting to me. I knew who I was and where I was going. I was building a life, one that didn't revolve around chasing shiny things. One with meaning and purpose. A real life. Our relationship had all the ingredients for something healthy and sustainable.

Or so I thought.

Like being in a riptide when you don't know how far out at sea you are, you don't realize how far you've drifted in a relationship until you do. There was nothing wrong or bad about our relationship. No one was at fault. There was no toxicity. No screaming matches, or fights, or infidelity. Just two people who were disconnecting from themselves.

As a therapist, I can tell you that there is always a reason for drift. I've wondered how much of the drift in this relationship was due to my two years of insomnia and depression from going through life like an exhaust pipe. I've wondered how much anger and resentment she carried for having put so much time into helping me build my business. And how thirsty I was for something more than toys and blindfolds in the bedroom. I knew something was wrong when she admitted that she didn't like my long hair anymore, but I also knew it wasn't about the hair. She and I both had always had trouble expressing how we felt. Even though I knew something was wrong with our relationship, though, I didn't work on it. I was tired. Becoming a better you suddenly felt like a billboard, one I didn't want to pass again. So I looked the other way.

The next thing I knew we were holding each other and sobbing uncontrollably because I was moving out. And in that moment, I thought to myself: *Is there a pattern here?* Did I always drift after two or three years in a relationship? Every relationship I'd been in seemed to last roughly three years, and I was always the one ending it. Was something deeper happening? Maybe I was comparing relationships to previous ones, or maybe I just didn't have what it took to be monogamous. Maybe I just chased the high, and when that faded I bounced. Was I a hypocrite? Was I full of shit? Or was it just that this was how my relationships had played out?

I know I was looking for a deeper intimacy, and she did admit that she struggled with providing more than skin. But that's all I knew. Anyway, I left. Again. Just like that. I was hoping she would beg me to stay, but she didn't. And I took that as a sign, which wasn't fair to her. I should have tried to work on it. But instead, I moved out. I ran. Later she told me that she thought it would be a trial separation and that I would come back. I didn't know this. I wonder if knowing that was her expectation would have made a difference.

Two weeks after I left, I ended up kissing another friend, one we both knew. She was a yoga "influencer" and made me feel desired again. I wasn't looking. We were both going through transitions and I felt connected to her. To be honest, I was lonely and looking for someone to validate me. I believe I blamed it on the full moon that night, but it was really my unwillingness to face hard things. Like being by myself. It was me taking the easier road.

And then suddenly I was in Hawaii, doing handstands on the beach and meeting the yoga friend's family. It was going too fast, and I wasn't ready for it. I was just chasing after approval and validation and the super-high of feeling desired, something I hadn't felt in a while. Of course when Patricia found out, the clouds of sadness parted, revealing a hurricane. Shit hit the fan times ten. I tried to make excuses because technically I was single. But it wasn't cool. Three years with someone deserves a courtesy period. And respect for the expired relationship before making out with a mutual friend on the beach on a weeknight. I knew this, but my behavior didn't line up.

The yoga girl and I only lasted a couple of months. After having my first panic attack one night from the guilt and anxiety of getting into something way too fast, and from the hurt it caused someone else, I thought it would be best if we went our separate ways. I needed to be alone. Again.

TIME TO MAKE SHIT HAPPEN

Like the twelve steps of Alcoholics Anonymous, there are necessary steps to declaring you are single. The purpose is not to advertise but to promise yourself that you will be a better person because of what happened. Single isn't just a status. Single is a choice to take your love lessons and grow.

Step 1: Accept That Your Relationship Has Expired

I know this sounds cold. Relationships are not milk. We're talking about a human who shared their heart with you. But this is more about a reframe, a mindset shift, a different way of looking at it to help you accept that the relationship is over and let go of it.

One of the hardest things about a breakup is wondering if it could have been different. *What if I did this? What if she was more like that? What if. . . . What if. . . .* The what-ifs keep us holding on, feeling like shit. We play back the highlight reel instead of the whole documentary. We drown in our emotions, questioning whether we made the right decision or could have done more. All these thoughts keep us stuck.

Your relationship has expired. It was not meant to last one day more or less. It has run its course. Not because of you or your partner, but for a different reason: your relationship hit its expiration date. You have to believe that.

Step 2: Cut the Cord

One of the greatest gifts my ex-wife gave me was a hard line in the sand. Firm boundaries. I didn't appreciate it at the time. She tapered off all communication, texts, emails, phone calls. It felt ice cold. I didn't understand how you could go from knowing each other for ten years to not knowing each other at all. But part of what felt "cold" came from being a boy who couldn't stand on his own. She needed the space and was protecting herself. Maybe for the first time in her life. She wanted to move through. And thank God, because I didn't have the strength to do it. I wanted to stay connected. To hold on to her leg and not let go. Her cutting of the cord forced me to go on my own journey.

There's no way around this one. You must unfriend, unfollow, and unsubscribe. Stop texting and calling. Resist the urge to leave voicemail. You have to let go. Maybe not forever. Maybe the two of you can be friends one day. But that won't come unless you give yourself space now. If you don't, you're just peeling scabs. You're holding two hostages: your ex, and you. Respect the relationship and what you had by respecting the expiration. Draw firm boundaries.

But what if you have a kid together?

You communicate. You get on the same page and establish healthy boundaries as best you can. It may get ugly. When we are hijacked by emotions, we may use our children as chess pieces. Even unintentionally. Our emotions are the elephant, our logic is the little rider on top, and the elephant is going to go where it's going to go. But it's critical that you set some kind of boundaries or healing won't happen. There's no way around it. Space is what heals. If you don't get it, you won't be moving through. Instead, you both will have shackles around your ankles from the residue of the relationship.

What if your ex doesn't want to communicate? Or just plays games? What if they're too angry? What if you're too angry?

Request a mediator or a couples counselor. Not to fix the relationship, but to help you both create healthy boundaries and respect each other while moving forward. Make sure these boundaries are crystal clear, or space will open up again for hurt, which will only lead to reactions. If you can't do it for yourself, do it for your child. Remind your ex of that as well.

Remember to pull from love, no matter how hard it is. No matter how angry or unsettled you are about what happened. Whether there was abuse, infidelity, or just the drifting apart of two people, don't live in what happened. Give yourself personal space to process and start healing so you don't get sucked back into the old relationship dynamic.

If you can't respect your ex, at least respect the expiration of the relationship. There is you. There is him or her. And there is what you guys built. It is a living breathing thing that has died. Respect that death by staying on your side of the fence. By not gossiping and lashing out. By not using your child as a tug-of-war rope. By drawing healthy boundaries.

Step 3: Take Ownership

This is the step we often forget. Or run from. But it's the most important one.

Most of us lay blame. We point our fingers and are quick to spell out everything our ex did wrong. This becomes a broken record that sinks us deeper. By blaming your ex, you are putting yourself in victim mode, as though you were powerless over what happened. And yes, many of us *have* been victims. If you've been in an abusive relationship, physical or emotional, you have been victimized.

Something has been taken from you. Self-esteem, voice, a sense of worth. And that wasn't your fault.

For many relationships, though, what happened is not so black-and-white. Sure, your partner was shitty sometimes, but were you perfect? Instead of feeling the pain of an expired relationship—and don't forget, a relationship always involves *two* people—it's easier to demonize your ex. This might feel good, but by ignoring your own role, you're setting yourself up for a repeat performance. By blaming and not taking any ownership, you are living in the past instead of creating the foundation for a better future.

The way you avoid history repeating itself is by taking ownership. That's how you get your power back. That's how you connect back to yourself. Without taking ownership, there is no growth, learning, or evolution.

I haven't always taken ownership. Instead of sitting with myself after the breakup with Street Art, I jumped into something new two weeks after, with someone she knew. I understand it happens all the time, and that's why people book sessions with me. But I don't believe in hurting people like that. I was lonely when I did that. I was also selfish and confused. And I was wrong.

When you own your part in the breakup, you can start growing again. You circle what happened with a red marker, but you also remind yourself that you're human. Taking ownership makes you accept the breakup, learn from it, and form a desire to be better. No space for growth can be created when you're defensive, make excuses, pull away from logic, and tell yourself and everyone else all the reasons why it wasn't your fault. You're running away from yourself instead of toward yourself. You're moving on, but you're not moving through.

Step 4: Focus on You

When a relationship expires, we want to jump into something else as fast as we can (speaking from experience). We search for our next ride right after getting off the last one, without giving ourselves any time to really process what happened and how we feel about it. Obviously, it's uncomfortable to be alone, and we want an easy fix. But love is not an amusement park. If you just keep jumping from one ride to the next, you will only repeat patterns. Nothing will change. I know I said it before but I'll say it again. The soil for growth is so rich when you're single. But only if you are focusing on you. Not on finding someone else.

Many don't know what to do with themselves when they are alone because they get their worth from loving someone else. They have never made life about themselves, but always about others. So they have never really built a relationship with themselves. They only know themselves *through* a relationship. And if those relationships have been unhealthy, their relationship with themselves has been unhealthy too. This is why it's so important to focus on you when you're single. You will also bring a more whole and authentic version of yourself to the table when you find someone who deserves you. The dynamic of the relationship will be different. It won't be like the last time.

So how do you do this? How do you focus on you? I bet if you hear "date yourself" one more time, you're going to jump off a building. Instead of thinking about going on sad dates with yourself, think about things that you've always wanted to do but didn't because you didn't have the time or the money, or you were afraid. Like traveling, picking up new hobbies, taking that Bollywood dance class you've had an eye on for so long. If saying yes to new experiences means "dating" yourself, then you should be dating yourself even when you are in a relationship.

But working on your relationship with yourself isn't just about *doing* things alone. It's about *being* alone. On purpose. Sitting with everything that comes up, however uncomfortable. Finally breaking the patterns you fall into to cope and numb when you are alone by noticing what comes up and why. This is the inner work. The hard work. This is what focusing on you looks like. This is where you build the relationship with yourself. It's an inside-out process, not an outside-in process. As you do this work, you also practice self-compassion and forgiveness. Accept your story, let go of what you need to let go of, and start leaning into your evolution.

Step 5: What Are Your New Non-Negotiables?

As you sit with yourself and with the uncomfortable, it's time to learn why you do what you do and where that comes from. And of course, it's also time to make a conscious effort to change those thoughts and behaviors and take a different path. As you start to play things back, take ownership of what has happened in your past and connect it back to yourself. (Remember, relationships, even healthy ones, can disconnect us from ourselves.) As you do this, you will start to draw new lines in the sand. You will create non-negotiables. Things that you will no longer tolerate because that shit didn't work any better the fourteenth time around than it did the first time. Remember: there's a difference between non-negotiables and preferences. Telling yourself you will date only men who are six-two, make six figures, and drive a vintage Porsche are not non-negotiables. That's called being picky. Non-negotiables are new standards you've created for yourself that line up with your new story. They form the container that houses and grows your sense of self-worth.

Here are some of my non-negotiables.

1. I will never be in an abusive relationship, neither physical nor emotional. I don't care if she blows my socks off and the chemistry is out of this universe. This is a very hard line.

2. I will not be with someone who does not support my passions or champion my story. She doesn't have to agree with me on everything or like the same things I like, but she has to support who I am and what I stand for.

3. I will not be with someone who does not take care of herself. This is not just about working out or maintaining a certain physical appearance. I will not be with someone who ignores her mental, emotional, physical, and spiritual health.

4. I will not be in a lopsided friendship. That's one where you always have to come to the other person, and where they always make it about them and never hold space for you. Friendships that are superficial.

Your non-negotiables don't all have to be big things. Needing to be able to have great banter with the other person can be a non-negotiable. They can be based on common interests and values. Maybe you will no longer tolerate being with someone who plays video games all day. Non-negotiables are not just for relationships and friendships. What are your non-negotiables at work? With family? When it comes to fitness? Or your home? What do you absolutely require with respect to nutrition and sleep? What will you never give up about your meditation practice?

Step 6: Smash the Clock

One of the most common questions people ask me after an expired relationship is: *How long does it take to get over someone?* Or: *It's been three months! Why am I still not over him?*

I hate to break it to you, but there is no fixed time it takes for you to "get over" someone. There is no formula, no secret steps. And just because you got over someone in three months last time doesn't mean it will take just as long this time. Here's the thing. Every relationship is different. They make imprints on us that vary in depth. Who you are or were in that relationship is different now. There are too many factors involved to be able to judge or compare your expired relationships this way. It's going to take as long as it's supposed to take to heal and move through.

Now Go Fuck Somebody

Let's assume that you have done some inner work. That you are already on a journey to self-growth and connecting back to yourself. That you have started the process of acceptance and taking ownership. That you have started grieving and allowing yourself to feel the loss of previous relationships. That you honestly feel like you're in a good place and ready to explore. And that you're not talking about involving someone in your social circle who is known to your ex. Assuming all these things, it may be time to go fuck somebody.

One thing I realized after my three-year relationship with Patricia ended was that I'd never really had the kind of singlehood experience most people have in their twenties. I'd always been in a relationship. Yes, I was single for a long stretch after my divorce, but I spent that time alone on a motorcycle, in front of a computer screen typing my feelings, or inside a CrossFit Box. I'd never had meaningless sex with someone I met at a bar, the kind you don't even remember when you wake up in the morning but you're okay with that because you just wanted a single-serving experience. I'd

147

never dated multiple people just to date, or dated with no intention of it "going somewhere." I'd never had a threesome, been to a sex party, or had a "friend with benefits."

I had usually hopped from one lily pad to another. I'd be single for a second, then meet someone, and suddenly we're splitting the rent and going to Trader Joe's on Tuesdays because Sunday's a shit show. Now, I understand that just fucking people doesn't lead to fulfillment. I know it leads to feelings of loneliness and to cravings for something deeper. It's not sustainable. I get it. But if you've never experienced it, it can become curious. Maybe it's a fantasy you wish you fulfilled long ago so you wouldn't have to wonder about it anymore. Maybe you feel the same way about drugs if you've never done them. (That's why I almost overdosed on mushrooms recently.) You get tired of feeling left out when people share stories.

I'm also advocating for you to go out and fuck someone because, besides satisfying your curiosity, we need to get rid of labels and shoulds. Sluts, whores, fuck boys, desperate, lonely—all of those labels are disruptive and dangerous, especially when we turn them inward and slap them on ourselves. What matters is the why, not the want. If you are sleeping with strangers because you don't want to be alone, or to seek validation of your worth and desirability, or in the hope that using sex as bait will turn an encounter into a relationship, you should not be having one-night stands every weekend. Because most likely you are repeating an unhealthy pattern and waking up in the morning feeling worse about yourself than before.

On the other hand, if you've been in nothing but relationships since high school and you're finally at a place where you're comfortable with your body and want to explore your sexuality, now is the time. Exploring your sexuality is in fact part of working on yourself. Our sexual need is a basic need. We are sexual beings. Most of us shelve that need when we get into a long-term relationship. Then we don't feed it when we're single because we're afraid the world will think we're slutty. But it's not about how many people you sleep with. It's about being in a healthy place when you sleep with other people.

If you've never had a one-night stand and you want to know what that feels like, then go fucking do it. I mean, be safe. Don't find someone on Craigslist. We don't want you to end up in a trunk. But if you're at a party or bar or even the grocery store and you strike up a conversation with someone and feel a spark, explore it. Feed that desire. It's okay. If you think someone is hot and want to share your body with them, go do it. If you want to know what sex feels like without commitment, give yourself that experience. If you want to have a threesome, use sex toys for the first time, or be with someone of the same sex, add that to your self-care list. Just make sure that you're being safe, that you've communicated so everyone's on the same page, and that your why is coming from a healthy place. **You're not fucking your feelings away. You are exploring your sexuality.** There is a huge difference.

"I Knew on My Wedding Day It Was a Mistake"

Stacey actually had an out. She was told by her best friend, "All you need to do is make eye contact with me, and I will grab your hand and we can pull a Thelma and Louise. Except for the ending. It will be like old times. Like we used to ditch Mrs. Carpenter's class!" But Stacey was not in high school anymore. She was thirty-two. And a cake had been ordered, a ring was on her finger, and over 150 people had made a commitment to celebrate what was supposed to be the happiest day of her life.

Stacey had been with her fiancé, Bob, for three years. The first year was great, like most first years are great. The high of discovering someone new. New arms to hold you. New takes on conversations. New restaurants to eat at. And finally, someone healthy, with emotional tools and consistency. Then Bob found God and became "super-religious." He decided he did not want to have sex anymore until they were married. So they didn't have sex for two years. The "great" faded to "good," then to "tolerable," and eventually to "He's like my brother. I feel zero chemistry with him." But she had already said yes. Besides, she was in her early thirties now and the thirties were for marriage, kids, and matching BMWs. Right? Deep inside, she did not believe that. She just didn't know anything different. She had only been in one other relationship, and it had been toxic and abusive. It was a pattern she needed to break, or her life would never get any better.

Stacey actually found me through Bob. He listened to my podcast religiously, read my books, even got my daily texts. He referred her to me because he thought I could "fix her." It's always a bad sign when someone sends their partner to me without coming along themselves. It's a move loaded with control and expectations, and it always backfires on the partner who stayed home. They don't realize how quickly their partner working on the relationship is about to out-grow them.

Therapists are not doctors. We don't "fix" anyone. We're more like fertilizer. We sit in shit all day and use it to help people grow. So knowing that Bob had referred Stacey to me made me nervous. I imagined him coming to me one day screaming, "You broke us up, you fucking fraud!" Thank God I don't have an office. He would have had to check every coffee shop in Los Angeles to find me. Anyway, this told me that she was going to leave him. It was just a matter of time. And of course, she did.

When that happened, I thought my work with Stacey was over. But it was just beginning. Now that she wasn't married to her "brother," she was free to do whatever (and whoever) she wanted. In the five years Stacey and Bob were together, they'd only had sex eleven times. That's 2.2 times a year! (I didn't say that out loud. I was just doing the math in my head.) She had also gained a lot of weight. It was what I call "hiding weight." Hiding from her problems, her misery, her husband, her self, and the world. But after she left him, she started to shed the weight, even though, she admitted, she didn't work out that much. It was almost like her body said, "Okay, let's do this," and started losing weight on its own. And she wasn't just literally lighter. Her energy was different. I told her what I tell all my clients going through expired relationships: "Out of your head, out of your house." But she didn't need that advice. She was always out and about. She was also going to grad school to study psychology. She had a new tribe. For me, it was like working with a brand-new person.

Once she was ready to date again—which was pretty much the day she ended her marriage—she got on dating apps. All of my other clients hated them, but Stacey had an entirely different experience. Dating apps empowered her. She used them as a tool. She had many suitors and started fucking different people. Not in a desperate "love me" way. She wasn't looking for love. She was exploring her new body and her sexuality. She wanted to taste all the flavors, color with more than one crayon. She'd never done that before. She now had the giant box with all forty-eight crayons. "I don't want to live not knowing anymore," she told me. She said that exploring her sexuality for the first time made her feel like a new woman.

I thought to myself, *Wow, I'll have what she's having.* As I mentioned earlier, I was a serial monogamist. I'd never gone through a period of intentional sexual exploration. But Stacey did, and it opened up a whole new world. Discovering she was desirable gave her more self-esteem and comfort and connection to her body. This led to confidence and an energy that attracted more men. All types of men. Bald, tall, short, strong, skinny, heavy, big penis, small penis. She was open and tossed away the idea that she had a "type." This was not about finding the one. It was about finding herself.

The focus of our conversations changed from sex and sexuality to social systems, relationship models, polyamory, and open relationships. She wondered if she could love more than one person. She wondered if she could be secure enough to not be jealous. She had never known she had a choice. She'd thought monogamous marriage was the only way. She also wasn't sure if she would want something other than monogamy if she fell madly in love with someone. She had so many questions. I started to have many questions myself.

Most people think that when they leave a session with their therapist changed and full of new insight, the therapist stays there like a revelation vending machine, just waiting for the next client to punch the machine and come in to receive new insights and revelations. But the truth is, therapists also have revelations and gain insight about our own lives during sessions and afterward. Sessions with our clients affect us as much as they affect our clients. Sometimes more.

It was time for me to go fuck somebody.

Dating Apps, DMs, and the First Time I Did Molly

Dating is like wanting to get to know your crazy uncle with the gold Trans Am better because you want to have your own experience with him and not believe what others say. Until you do get to know him and you're like, oh.

I was single again, and this time I was telling myself I was going to date, really date. Not jump into a relationship with the first person I had a connection with. That seemed to be the pattern in my life. Meet someone, feel something, and suddenly we're sharing bath towels and walking on eggshells. Let's break it down.

My first real relationship was a three-year deal in my early twenties. Tons of codependency. An abortion. And as I found out twenty years later after randomly running into her at an Al-Anon meeting, she had kissed someone else at a concert. The next relationship was a five-year deal that turned into a five-year marriage. This was the big one. More codependency. Unhealthy intimacy. Putting her on a pedestal. Me going from her mouth to her nipple. Possible sex and/or love addiction. Completely losing myself. After the divorce, there was another three-year deal, this time around with the Tumblr girl from Georgia. I was controlling, ambivalent, and unhappy with my life, as she told me herself at the time but I didn't believe it. Then Street Art, my *When Harry Met Sally* experience, the friend turned lover. Another three-year deal. Best friends. Great banter. Workouts. Making art together. Sex toys for the first time. The first taste of a healthier love. But you see the pattern here? Jumping from one lily pad to another, up until my early forties.

I'm not in the 100s club like most of my male friends. I haven't had many sexual experiences. So when that last relationship ended, I wanted to explore. Taste the rainbow, if you will. Channel my inner Stacey and her sixty-four-crayon box. Maybe even have a one-night stand, something I'd never done before.

So I started "dating." I got on the apps. Put myself out there. Got out of my head and my house. This led to coffee dates, learning what being catfished meant, realizing that no one looks like their photos, and not being able to get it up three times in a row with a girl from San Diego. (That still bothers me!) Long story short, I was going through a period of low testosterone and instead of listening to and taking care of my body, I was trying to force things. And the more I tried to "give myself a new experience" the more shame I felt for not being able to. Because I, like many men, have been programmed to tie manhood to performance. I'm not going to lie. It's still something I wish I could go back and change. I want another at-bat, a second chance to knock it out of the park. But maybe the lesson is to listen to my penis. It knows things as well.

Shortly after that encounter, I did Molly for the first time with someone I met on Instagram. I'd always heard stories about how Ecstasy makes you feel when you're having sex but never tried it. I hadn't done any drugs really, save the one time an ex-girlfriend and I nearly died overdosing on edibles. (It was at the peak of my insomnia, and I had no idea eating half a brownie and three chews was the equivalent of smoking eight joints.)

The Molly experience started as a friendly coffee date that didn't really go anywhere. I thought she was cute, but I wasn't looking for love. A few weeks after our coffee date, I told her I'd never done Molly and asked her if she wanted to try it with me. She was down. Came over with orange juice and vitamins to make sure I would be okay the next day, since many people get depressed coming down from it. I thought that was very sweet. But there was no rave or shower sex. It was actually a very sweet innocent experience. It was like Molly for Dummies, Ecstasy 101. Not the "waking up half-naked facedown in an abandoned warehouse" experience I had kind of hoped for. We had a salad, listened to music, and fooled around like we were at summer camp. It was innocent and sweet, the PG version of *Sex on Molly*. We went on a handful of dates after that, but then I met someone I started seeing seriously and that pretty much ended my "wild single-hood in my twenties I never experienced but want to" experiment. I know. No sex parties. No threesomes. No waking up next to someone I wanted out of my bed. Oh well. I tried.

I was wishing I had explored more. But I guess I just wasn't meant to have those kinds of experiences. And life never delivers what we imagine in our head anyway. Still, as short-lived as my dating era was, it did make me stretch and learn about different sexual energy and connections. It made me understand myself better. That's the important piece: understanding yourself better. I believe the experience gave me a sharper radar. Because it's never about the sex. It's about giving yourself new experiences so you can discover what you want and don't want, what works for you and what doesn't, what you like and don't like. How something makes your body feel. How someone else makes you feel. How you want to be treated. It's all about learning more about yourself.

I learned that I'm not a dater, that I'm the happiest when I'm in a monogamous relationship, and that's okay. I like thinking about one person and building something with that person. I learned that discovering someone new is exciting, but that the best sex and the deepest intimacy come from exploring with one person for a long time. At forty-six, I'm interested in a deeper love, not just sex, and I don't believe you can get that by dating many people. I don't know about tomorrow. Five years from now, I may be in five relationships at once and two of them may be men. I don't know. But today this is my truth. And you can't get to your truth unless you are always searching, exploring, and discovering. That's what building a relationship with yourself looks like.

If you're in a monogamous relationship, the process is still the same and you don't need an entire box of crayons. You just need one, along with the courage to be honest by sharing your desires and needs. Communication isn't just about feelings. What's stirring inside you? What are you curious about? How do you want to be loved, explored, desired? How do you want to be touched that's different and new? Do you want to bring toys into the bedroom? Act out a fantasy? It's not about fucking somebody. It's about rediscovering yourself through new experiences that change your definitions. And you can do that with your partner. New experiences will bring the two of you closer together and make it less tempting to look over the fence at other people's lawns.

TIME TO MAKE SHIT HAPPEN

Your Sex Life Starts with You. Always.

Before we get to everything your partner *isn't* doing, ask yourself if you feel sexy as an individual. Without your partner. Or when you're surrounded by your "hot" friends. Just you. No sexy dress. Standing in front of a mirror. Barefoot and naked. Are you okay with what you see? Or do you cringe and bash yourself? Because sexy isn't just about your body. It's about your relationship with yourself.

If you don't feel sexy today, when's the last time you did? Before the crazy job that now leaves you with just enough energy to put on pajamas when you get home? Before you got married? Before the kids came? Before the accident? Or did it slowly burn off? Like Stacey, did you gradually numb yourself with food to hide and not face your unhappiness? Sexy runs deeper than what your body looks like. Sexy is a mindset, an attitude, a journey that requires you to know, love, and accept yourself as you push and build yourself.

Imagine that you have four pistons, like a car. And the more they are pumping, the more you are connecting to yourself, aka feeling whole, complete, and ultimately like a sexual being. Most of us have only a couple of pistons pumping. Because life happens and we forget to work on maintaining them at peak function. Like an engine, you stop moving forward when your pistons stop pumping. Your growth stops. Your evolution stops. Your sexy stops.

Let's run through these. Ask yourself which pistons you need to get pumping again.

THE FIRST PISTON

Two things I've mentioned elsewhere apply here as well: moving your body and liking yourself.

Although I've always been a highly sexual person, I don't know if I ever actually felt sexy until I started moving my body. Yes, CrossFit gave me two and a half abs and a rounder butt, but it was the connection to myself—the comfort with self through movement— that made me feel sexier. It was the first time I actually enjoyed working out. I'd worked out before and had been lifting weights since high school, but always for aesthetic reasons, not because I liked it. It wasn't until I found something I actually loved that I was able to drop into my body and push it harder than I ever had before, which dissolved some of my false beliefs. This was when I started to build a real relationship with my body. Not a superficial one.

That's the key piece: building a relationship with your body based on substance, not the superficial. Substance is where sexy is born. If you're just going through the motions or moving for someone else, the relationship you build with your body will be superficial and most likely short-lived. People build authentic relationships with their bodies when they fall in love with the movement so much that it becomes a lifestyle. Yoga. Running. Skating. Rock climbing. Any movement that produces dopamine but also requires discipline. Any movement that becomes a part of your daily life because you love doing it so much.

THE SECOND PISTON

Do you like who you are as a person? I'm talking about your character. Your values. Your gifts. Your story. Having a strong sense of self.

I didn't like myself for most of my adult life. I tied my worth to what I did, and since I wasn't "successful," I didn't feel like I had much worth. I didn't have values, character, or a strong why. I just spent a lot of time in coffee shops writing screenplays and hoping I could sell them so I would be worth something. It wasn't until I changed careers and started a new life and a new relationship with myself that I began to like myself. I started liking myself only when I started listening to myself, treating myself better, and practicing self-compassion, self-care, and self-discipline, all of which shaped my character. It wasn't until I finally allowed myself to know me that I started to like me. But like building any relationship, the dance of liking yourself is a lifelong process. What's important is getting it started. Because if you don't like yourself, it's impossible to feel sexy. Again, you can present yourself as sexy, especially if you've been blessed with good genes, but you can't truly feel a core-deep sexy that moves from the inside outward. That comes from liking yourself.

THE THIRD PISTON

Many of us grow up being taught that sex is bad and sinful. So we feel shame and guilt for exploring our bodies and having sexual thoughts and feelings. We shut it down. By doing this, though, we are blocking an important part of ourselves. We are all sexual beings, just as we are spiritual beings. If we ignore or suppress that part, we are disconnecting from ourselves and making it impossible to feel sexy. Because our sexy has become lined with shame, the lowest life frequency, and sexy and shame cannot coexist.

It's time to scrap shame by accepting that you are a sexual being and that it's okay to express yourself in a sexual way. What would that look like for you in action? Wearing clothes that make you feel sexy? Talking about sex and what you like in the bedroom with your partner? Having multiple partners (as long as you're communicating and everyone's on the same page)? Going home with someone you just met and not feeling bad about it? Masturbating more? Using toys with your partner? Trying different locations? Role-play? Sex dungeons? Playing out fantasies? Doing Molly with someone you met on the internet?

Or . . .

Maybe for you acceptance of your sexuality means abstaining for now. Not having sex for a while. Maybe sex has become the barrier to intimacy. Yes, you read that right. Maybe you're fucking your feelings. Using sex as a shield to hide behind your fear of revealing too much of yourself and fear of getting to know someone on a deeper level. Maybe you didn't know this because you thought the act of sex meant connection. As long as you were having sex, you were connecting with someone. But you have never had that connection to yourself. You've been connecting to everyone else. Maybe it's time to rediscover sex and what it means for you. Maybe it's time to put down your shield.

THE FOURTH PISTON

Do you feel sexy?

We are sexual beings. The need to feel sexy is in our DNA, in our wiring, in the fabric of who we are. Feeling sexy is not extra or optional, not just something that happens when we fit into a tight dress or get a compliment from a stranger. Sexy is a basic human need. Like food, water, and sleep. And the only person who can fulfill that need is you. You must feed your sexual need daily or you will feel incomplete. Invisible. Not feeding it will directly impact whoever you choose to love. You will minimize, compromise, refuse to believe you deserve better.

How are you feeding your need to feel sexy?

Here's how I currently feed my sexual need.

Daily Sweat. I work out daily and switch it up by taking various classes so I'm not always doing the same movements and workouts. I listen to my body and do what it craves. But I also follow a program (which classes provide) so I have structure and goals. I'm not just doing what I feel like doing. Sometimes I get outside and go for a hike, run, or swim. Also, I rarely work out alone. I use communities to push me and make me accountable but also to meet my social need. Killing two birds with one stone. Through working out and movement, I build a better relationship with my body. I relieve stress, burn fat, and build muscle, but most important, I feel more comfortable in my body. That leads to feeling more whole, more confident, and, ultimately, more sexy.

Motorcycle Rides. When I ride my motorcycle, I feel completely free and present. My senses are heightened, I forget about all my problems, and I remember being a kid, without a worry in the world. Riding connects me to my inner child who didn't care what anyone thought about him. He just did things that pumped adrenaline through his veins and dopamine in his head. That's a state that makes me feel fearless, and when I feel fearless, I feel sexy. A motorcycle gives me that feeling. I try to ride a few times a week. I take long rides, short rides, along the beach, hugging canyons—

wherever I go on my bike I feel more alive. And anything that makes you feel alive can also make you feel sexy.

Sex. Yes, I try to have sex as much as I can, but it's not just about the amount of sex. It's about how you feel about yourself and in your body during sex. Are you even enjoying it? Many people have sex just to make the other person happy. Sex can become routine and mechanical, especially in long-term relationships. Sex can be about pleasing someone else.

One of the greatest misconceptions about healthy sex is that you don't need to put any work into it. That it's a natural act. You just get naked and it's all good. That's not true, though. You have to work on sex. I start with communication. I try to tell my partner what I like and don't like and encourage her to do the same. I explore. Switch it up. Play out my fantasies. My partner's fantasies. Try things I may have labeled or judged. I try to see sex as a form of self-expression. Not just a means to having an orgasm. Sex is a shared space where you get to know and connect to another person but also to yourself. And the more you do that, the more you are fulfilling your sexual need and the sexier you feel.

Masturbation. Replace the word "masturbation" with "self-exploration" if you want. Many people, especially men, masturbate to relieve their pent-up sexual energy. They masturbate to finish, to release, to feel good. And that's okay. Keep it up. But masturbation can be more than that. It can be a way to know yourself. Our bodies change. How we feel in our bodies changes. What turns us on changes. Masturbation can be a way to connect to yourself and your desires. So use it to explore, not just to "rub one out."

I'm not going to lie. Of course I masturbate if my partner isn't in the mood or I feel horny and want to release. But I also use it to explore my body, to get comfortable with myself, to discover new likes and how I want to be touched. I use it to check in with myself and my sexual needs.

I also masturbate with my partner. We do it not just to see, and show, exactly how we like to be touched but also as an exercise to build trust. It's an intimate experience people rarely share with each other. It's difficult to show and express yourself in that way without feeling self-conscious. But the more trust you and your partner build, the safer the space for the two of you to explore your sexiness. Masturbation can be a shared experience that makes both people feel sexy.

How many of the four pistons—moving your body, liking yourself, scrapping shame, and feeding your sexual need—are pumping in your life today? If none of them are, your engine has stalled out. That means you are not thriving and not connecting to yourself. Focus on each piston and make sure to get them all pumping. Some may be pumping faster than others, but that's okay. Just make sure you are paying attention to all of these pistons and making an effort to work on each one. Remember, it's a process, and it gets easier the more you practice it. But to keep your pistons pumping, they must be threaded into your daily life as your lifestyle, not just as a once-in-a-while thing.

One of the Most Common Mistakes in Relationships

When we're single and working on ourselves, it's easier to get the four pistons pumping. We work out hard. We eat better. We make sure we look and feel good. We do our hair. We put effort into what we wear. Our socks go with our outfits. Since we don't want to be single forever, we make sure we're looking and feeling the best that we can. Inside and out. We do our best to build a sense of confidence and to feel sexy. Then we get into a relationship and all that goes out the window.

Maybe we don't slack off the first month. But over time we start working out less. Putting less effort into what we wear and what we look like. Go back to our poor eating habits. Discover our socks are mismatched and don't give a fuck. Why should we? We're not looking anymore. We have a partner now. And that partner has to sleep with us because they love us. Besides, they should accept us for us, right? Wrong.

When you're in a relationship, you have a responsibility to continue to take care of yourself, and feeling confident and sexy is part of that. That is *your* responsibility, not your partner's. Yes, that person may love you, but remember: love is a choice. Your partner is choosing to love you, but that doesn't mean they find you just as attractive as they did at first. You should not stop doing everything you were doing to take care of yourself when you got into the relationship. You should actually be doing more.

Just as we're responsible for our own happiness in our relationship, we are also responsible for how we look and feel about ourselves. That is *not* your partner's responsibility. Many of us fall into that trap. We think that because we are now in a relationship, our work on ourselves can stop or slow down. Why does this create drift and disconnect? **Because it's not just how you look and feel that becomes unattractive, but the fact that you don't care about how you look and feel.** Neglecting your appearance can flip the switch and change the entire dynamic of the relationship. Remember, attraction is not a constant. If you want your partner to continue to be attracted to you, you have to continue to work on being attractive.

That's why it's important to lay these tracks when you're single and build up some momentum by making every aspect of self-care part of your daily routine. The more confident and connected you feel to yourself now, the more you will be bringing to the table in your next relationship and the less pressure you will put on your partner and the relationship to make you feel better about yourself. You're not taking care of yourself for someone else. You are taking care of yourself for you. Everything ripples out from that.

ACT III

The New You

Closure Isn't
What You Think It Is

Closure happens right after you accept that letting go and moving on is more important than projecting a fantasy of how the situation could have been.

—SYLVESTER MCNUTT III

Social psychologist Arie Kruglanski started using the phrase "need for closure" in the 1990s. He was "referring to a framework for decision making," a *Psychology Today* writer explained in 2018, "that aims to find an answer on a given topic that will alleviate confusion and ambiguity." Quoting Kruglanski, the article continues: "When we seek closure, we are looking for answers as to the cause of a certain loss in order to resolve the painful feelings it has created." In doing this, "we appear to form a mental puzzle of what's happened—examining each piece and its relationship to the overall puzzle." Closure is achieved "when we are satisfied that the puzzle has been assembled to our satisfaction, that the answers have been reached and it is, therefore, possible to move on."

Lack of closure can keep us stuck. It's the giant brick wall that prevents us from getting through to the other side. We desperately search for answers as to why something ended. We try to make sense of it, and if we can't, we stay trapped on the wrong side of that brick wall. Seeking a puzzle piece that someone else is holding, we can't escape the past. This causes us to hold grudges, harbor resentment, and question our worth. If we can't find closure, we don't allow ourselves to let go and actually live in the present.

Here's a scene from a session with a client who was stuck because she needed closure.

A TRENDY COFFEE SHOP SOMEWHERE IN LOS ANGELES
John sits with his client, Amanda, who's in her early thirties. She's wiping croissant flakes off her shirt.

AMANDA
God, I'm a mess.

JOHN
Yeah, pastries are my weakness too.

AMANDA
If I could stop eating bread, my life would be perfect. Seriously.

JOHN
How's it going with Steve?

AMANDA

He cheated on me.

JOHN

Oh. I'm sorry.

AMANDA

Whatever. He was vegan. I wasn't even that into him.
(*She actually was.*) I don't know why I keep attracting
douchebags! Are there any faithful men in this world?
It's these fucking croissants. I've gained twenty pounds!

JOHN

You think it's your weight?

AMANDA

Men like skinny bitches. (*She takes another bite of her
croissant.*) I don't even care. I just want to know why.

JOHN

What does it mean to you to find out why he cheated?

AMANDA

What do you mean?

JOHN

There's a pattern here. You also didn't get an answer
from your fiancé.

AMANDA

Doesn't everyone want to know why?

JOHN

What if you found out that Kyle cheating on you had nothing to do with you? That it had to do with him escaping or hiding or running or maybe being afraid of marriage or not wanting to work on the relationship?

AMANDA (*after thinking about this for a long second*)

Well, then it would mean it wasn't my fault.

JOHN

And what would that mean?

AMANDA (*looking out the window as tears well*)

That I'm not a piece of shit.

Amanda attached the cheating to her worth. She needed to know why men cheated on her because, if it wasn't her fault, it meant she wasn't defective, she had value, she was a good partner, and she was lovable. But most important, it would mean she wasn't like her mother, for whom she had no respect. Her mother was cheated on by her father multiple times. She was also abusive to Amanda and her sisters and had very low self-esteem. One of Amanda's greatest fears was that she would end up like her mom. So when men cheated on her, she placed herself in the same category as her mom.

As we worked together, Amanda realized that subconsciously she picked men who would cheat on her. She was reenacting what felt familiar while growing up. Like her mother, deep inside Amanda didn't believe she had worth. Once we worked on her self-esteem and separated her worth from the unfaithful men in her life, she was able to see that men cheating on her had nothing to do with her value as a person. She was able to separate herself from her mother and finally start letting go and moving through. Most important, she learned that she didn't need answers and explanations from her exes to do any of this. All she needed was to know where her own desire to know was coming from and why it was so important to her.

The Surface Is Glass

Monica made it easy for me. She wouldn't let me talk, which I do way too much of as a therapist. She wanted to lay it all out first like a giant jigsaw puzzle. There was so much happening all at once for her, as there always is in life. She had recently answered her internal call to live near water and moved out to California. She had always dreamed of doing that, but had always been afraid to follow through. Or maybe she just needed a reason. She was stuck in a marriage that wasn't going anywhere for years, and she had finally mustered the courage to leave. But her departure triggered her ex-husband's internal collapse. He wasn't emotionally stable, so she couldn't really cut the cord. So it stretched. Creating anxiety and guilt. She would call her ex daily to check up on him while also trying to be present with a new person she had started dating. That was puzzle piece number one.

The person she was dating was also friends with her ex-husband. That was puzzle piece number two. She was also being harassed at work by someone who had trouble with boundaries (puzzle piece number three). Then there was her living situation. She had just been evicted because she had taken in a rescue cat (puzzle piece number four).

All in all, after Monica had laid it all out, there were about ten pieces. I lost count, but that didn't matter. What did matter was her false belief that love doesn't last. This belief became imprinted after her mom cheated on her dad, causing her parents to divorce when she was ten. Since then, she had always been afraid to go "all in." On the surface, she couldn't pry herself away from her ex-husband because he was unstable. There was truth and honest compassion there. But I wondered if unconsciously she was using her ex's dependency as a reason to not fully show herself and lean into the new person she was dating. She really saw a future with him, and that can be terrifying for someone who believes that love doesn't last.

Once she realized this, she knew she had to fully cut the cord with her ex-husband so that she could be present and create a new love experience that would prove her false belief wrong. Of course there were no guarantees this would happen, but if she wasn't even present, she wouldn't be giving this new relationship a fair shot, and the chances of it not working out would be high—once again cementing her false belief and fortifying the wall around her heart.

After a few weeks, she stopped taking care of her ex-husband and finally broke off ties with him. This was one of the hardest things she ever had to do. But with it came growth and a chance at a new love experience, one that could create new tracks and start to dissolve false beliefs.

We all have underlying patterns. Once we realize what they are, what's really going on, we can break unhealthy patterns and start to grow. We can make choices we didn't see before and now have leverage we didn't have before because it was buried. You can't get traction keeping things at surface level. The surface is glass. What's happening underneath is what really matters.

"Closure" requires nothing from the other person involved. It does not require an answer, an apology, or an explanation. If it did, very few people would truly be able to move on because most relationships end unsettled and unresolved. Rarely do we get to sit down with our exes and explain ourselves. Breakups have messy endings, and the only thing you can do about it is explore your own self. This is where you will find closure. But closure is not a situation where one door needs to close in order for another to open. Closure is a process. It is a journey. Some days you will reflect on what happened and have strong feelings about it. On other days you won't. As with any loss, the intensity of your feelings will go up and down and those feelings will come and go. Until they go more than they come.

Nothing is ever truly closed. You will always remember, and you will have feelings attached to those memories. But the feelings can change as you embark on the journey of closure, which will take you inward to explore your self and to grow. If your feelings do not change, you'll carry the residue of what happened, harboring hate, anger, and resentment. Not only toward your ex but maybe also toward yourself. This will harden you, and that energy will ripple into your other relationships. You won't be able to create a brand-new love experience because you will be painting on a stained canvas.

The Dog Died → I Finally Sat Down with My Ex-Wife → I Put My Hair Away

Before theangrytherapist@gmail, I was brasschucky @gmail. Chucky was my American name because teachers couldn't pronounce Chul-Ki (which I recently found out my parents spelled wrong). Anyway, it was an old email used by the previous me. I wanted nothing to do with it, so I never checked it. But one day I did (I can't remember why) and scrolled through the in-box. There was nothing but spam. Then I saw an email from my ex-wife, someone I had not had contact with in nearly a decade. It was so random that I saw it, pure coincidence that I was checking it that day, a needle in a haystack. She emailed me to notify me that her/our dog had died. Natural causes, after living a full life. The news kind of shocked me and made me realize how long it had been. I asked if we could meet up.

I had been wanting to sit down with my ex-wife. Not to bring shit up, but because I just never felt closure with the divorce. It had felt sudden, like a car accident that gave me a ten-year whiplash. So here it was. Our first meeting in nearly a decade.

We went to get Korean barbecue. The first thing she said when she saw me was, "Well, you look different." Nothing else. I was sure it was my long hair. She looked confused as I scrambled off to the restroom to tie it into a man bun. (Yes, I was that guy.) I came back. We chatted. Had a few laughs. Nothing heavy, nothing about the past. It went by in a flash. The only thing I really remember about that night was that she gave me a real hug when we were waiting for our cars at the valet. A knowing hug that implied *We've been through a lot together and all is forgiven.* It made me feel like there was closure. Like reaching the period after a long run-on sentence. The end.

Well, not exactly. Getting that email had shaken me. It made me realize how much I'd hurt her. It made me wonder if there was more to our story than my version. I questioned myself and my memory. Then seeing her moved me emotionally. It sparked old feelings again. I missed her dad. And our dog. It didn't help that she had ended that email with "I love you." Deep inside, I knew what she meant. She meant *I love you as a person who was in my life once.* But Chul-Ki wanted to believe there was more. So I contacted her again, invited her to CrossFit. She had no idea what that was. We went back and forth a bit. Then I sent her a message letting her know that I got a haircut and that seeing her had brought up some feelings I didn't know were there. She shut that shit down real quick. She didn't want me to contact her anymore.

A few months later, I went on that dirt bike trip and

wanted to share a video with her dad, since we had motorcycles in common. I thought he would dig it. Was this Chul-Ki again, looking for a way in? I don't know. Most likely. So I texted her a video to show him. I won't get into what she said back, but it was pretty shocking and really confusing since our dinner had seemed calm and friendly. She was obviously still very angry about the past and what I took from her. I decided not to be defensive, admitted that I was a "piece of shit" then, and promised myself I would never contact her again, which I haven't.

Sometimes this is what closure or moving through looks like. You have no control over the other person and their experience of you or what happened. And if your definition of closure is making sure they see things like you do, they're okay with things, and they're not mad at you anymore, you will never move on. Closure means making a decision to let go of their journey and focus on your own. And also not checking old email accounts.

Maybe I hadn't fully grieved the loss. And maybe she hadn't either. I don't know. Because there is no time line or finish line with closure. Feelings come and go, until they don't one day. And then they come back again, triggered by something in your life. But the intensity lessens and the gap widens, and that's how you know you have allowed yourself to feel new things. But it is still a process, and it may take a lifetime.

Closure is not a door. It is a bridge. To a new and better "less shit-carrying more living in the present with more capacity to love" you.

Since you don't need anyone else to get closure, there's no need to wait another minute. *First,* ask yourself what you are holding on to from previous relationships. Especially if you're in a relationship now. Do you need an apology, an explanation like Amanda did? Do you need to know that it wasn't your fault? What exactly is it that you need to truly move forward? Because holding on to that will prevent you from being present. If you went through an expired relationship, wanting that puzzle piece from the other person— whatever it is you don't have closure on—so that things will make sense to you or make you feel better about yourself is keeping you from thriving and connecting to yourself. Needing that puzzle piece is making you less whole and making you dependent on something you may never get. It's a thorn in your side. A stone in your shoe. What are you holding on to?

Second, ask yourself *why* you need this. Usually what we believe we need from someone else is tightly tied to a belief about ourselves. About our worth. Or our ability to love. It's the proof that we are attractive or lovable. It's never about being right or just wanting to know. That's only on the surface. There's always something deeper attached. That's why you want it so much and it's so hard to let go of.

Third, whatever this need is tied to, can you give that to yourself instead? Using Amanda's example, she needed to get to a place where she believed she had value. She needed to believe that men cheating on her wasn't about her. She needed to become aware that she was picking this type of man to be with and she needed to stop doing that. But she needed to establish a better relationship with herself first. By doing so, she would stop choosing men who would be unfaithful. Only then could she set herself up for a new love experience that would make her feel valuable and worthy. Addressing these needs was something she could give to herself.

Of course it would require a journey. But she didn't need anything from her exes. She didn't need an explanation from them, as she had thought. She was holding the missing puzzle piece the entire time. So are you.

What *I* needed was an identity. I had lost it in my marriage. I had no sense of self. No life direction. I was the guy married to *her*. That's it. That's all I was. So I held on to the marriage because, without it, I didn't know who I was. And since I didn't know who I was and had no sense of self, I didn't feel like I had any value. Because of my low self-worth, I put her up on a pedestal. She was "out of my league." That made her a trophy, not a wife. And without her, I was worth less. Closure to me meant finding an identity and building a sense of worth. It took me nearly a decade and a total rebirth. But new definitions come with a new sense of self. And that's when your life can really change.

"Do You Date White Girls?"

He runs up to me like he forgot it was my birthday. "Do you date white girls?" I pause for a second, partly confused, partly insulted. I wasn't sure if it was a racist joke or if he was being serious. I reply, "That's pretty much all I've dated, dude." He says, "Great, I have a friend for you. She's a therapist!" Again, confused and insulted. Does he think therapists only date therapists? "Jason, what are you on today?"

He tells me her name is Vanessa. He used to do projects with her in New York. She went from corporate work in advertising and producing in New York to yoga, mindfulness, and working as a therapist in Los Angeles. He and Vanessa had recently gone on a hike to catch up and he mentioned me. I actually appreciated that he tried to set me up. It was a sweet gesture, and a rare way to meet someone in today's swipe culture. I'd never gone on a blind date before.

So after stalking the shit out of her Instagram, I asked Vanessa to meet me at a place called Little Dom's, a cozy Italian restaurant I could literally hit with a quarter from my bedroom window. It wasn't that I was lazy. Little Dom's is one of my favorite spots. It just happened to be right next door to my place. There's a huge difference between lazy and convenient!

Anyway, I was pleasantly surprised. Vanessa looked even better in person. It's usually the other way around. And we spoke the same language. I could tell she had been through some dark tunnels and was on a spiritual journey of self-betterment. But again, I didn't want to jump into anything. I still wanted to explore and date. No slipping into three-year deals anymore. For a little while at least, I was planning on pulling a Clooney—minus the good looks, fame, and house in Italy of course. I had no plans on getting into another relationship.

Flash-Forward:

More dates involving food.

A motorcycle ride.

A trip to Costa Rica.

A retreat in Joshua Tree.

Suddenly I'm in a relationship.

There was resistance from me, and she felt it. My energy was ambivalent. I went back and forth, hot and cold. I was afraid to go all in. I felt like the bases were loaded and this was my last at-bat. My next relationship was going to be my last one. So I was putting a lot of pressure on myself, on her, and on our connection. I took a black light to us. I questioned our differences, of which there were many. She's an extrovert. I'm an introvert. She colors inside the lines. I have no lines. She is very organized. I am a walking tornado.

I think I was looking for the perfect pitch, or the lightning in the bottle. But what I realized was that I was trying to trace an old love imprint—that feeling twenty-five-year-old me had when my ex-wife walked into my family's restaurant bar looking for a job. I saw an angel that day, and I think subconsciously, in all my relationships, I'd been chasing that angel ever since. Not her, but the feeling. That pursuit had been running underneath, in my river of subconscious. I realized it had kept me from exploring and growing in love. When we chase old feelings, experiences, and definitions, we are not allowing new ones in. I hadn't been aware of being stuck in old ways of loving. Until now.

But here's the thing. When you pull the curtain back and start playing back the documentary instead of the highlight reel, the "angel" turns into a demon pretty quickly. That "lightning" is followed by the thunder of dysfunction. Those feelings may be powerful and real, but are they healthy? Of course not. Young love rarely is. Sure, the attraction is real. But it's also produced by your wiring, by childhood trauma, by commercials. Young love is new love, and any new experience will be the most powerful a young person has ever had.

Once I realized this, I could finally give Vanessa and me a fair shot. I could now try to love *without* my past. I could stop comparing. Stop tracing. And when I started being present instead, I discovered a new soul and a brand-new love experience.

Some of My New Definitions of Love

BEAUTY

I used to think beauty was purely physical. That it was about body, eyes, and curves. I associated beauty with what I saw in magazines and tied it to my worth. The more commercially beautiful my girlfriend was, the more value I believed I had. Beauty was the antidote for everything I was lacking inside. But as I started to connect more to myself, discovering a sense of self and worth, my definition of beauty changed. It went from two-dimensional to four-dimensional. When I went from seeing beauty in a cardboard cutout to recognizing it in a real person, I was able to *feel* beauty instead of just seeing it.

For me today, beauty is no longer skin-deep. Beauty is about soul and capacity. It starts with kindness. Without kindness, it's all just makeup to me. Beauty is about not being judgmental, about depth, about awareness of self and your effect on others through your words and actions. It's about thoughtfulness, support, communication, banter, eye contact. Beauty lies in having your own life. In love and appreciation for your body, in having an open mind, in being open to different perspectives and opinions, in trying to understand before trying to be understood. Beauty is being gentle but strong, careful with your words, and able to forgive right away instead of holding on to resentment. Beauty is honest and consistent communication. Beauty is not complaining, not seeing yourself as a victim, not making everything about you. Beauty is lining up your actions with your words, practicing gratitude and compassion, believing in things greater than yourself, standing for something, giving people the benefit of the doubt even though you've been hurt many times. Beauty is also being able to draw strong healthy boundaries with a Sharpie instead of chalk. Beauty is the fire in your belly flamed daily by action. Beauty is vulnerability, commitment, consistency, communication, standing in your truth. Beauty is responding instead of reacting. Beauty is leaning into and growing through life's turbulence. Beauty is being able to look inward and love hard by loving responsibly.

ATTRACTION

I used to believe that love was only about lightning sparks. That whole "locking eyes across the room and just knowing" dynamic. But that's not love. That's a fairy tale. And most likely dysfunction. It's usually a sticky relationship dynamic that stems from trauma and old wounds. Just because it feels familiar doesn't mean it's love. Love is not about the old. Love is about the new. And love takes time. It requires a peeling of the layers. Love becomes a process. It starts with a daily choice. Then action to back up that choice. Some days love is easy. Some days it's hard. Love fluctuates. It's a dance, with an ebb and flow. Love is not a constant. And it changes daily. Attraction is a flash in the pan. Love will be around long after those flames burn out.

WHERE LOVE IS FOUND

Love is found in moments. The moment when you realize you were heard. Maybe for the first time. The moment you realize he's not trying to change you. The moment at the counter eating pancakes for dinner after a quickie and you think to yourself, *I like myself right now*. The moment when he finally puts the dishes away. That moment when you guys are on the couch doing nothing and you realize there's nothing you'd rather be doing. That moment when you *don't* laugh together at the joke. The moment after a fight when you guys come back together and the relationship just got stronger. That moment when you feel her touch and you'd recognize it even if you were blindfolded. That moment when you realize this one is different. That moment when you realize you had to swim past the breakers to find calm. The moment you see home in your partner's eyes.

It doesn't matter which door you enter. You can create new definitions so you can give yourself new experiences. Or you can give yourself new experiences so you can create new definitions. Either way, what's important is that you break old patterns. It's old patterns that keep us locked. New experiences and definitions break that lock by creating new thoughts and behaviors, leading you to different choices and ultimately a different relationship with yourself. A better relationship. One that's stronger and more authentic and closer to your truth and who you want to be. This is how you shed old definitions and old patterns. This is how you evolve. This is how you bring more to the table when you do find someone who deserves you.

If you don't create a new definition of love, you will always attract and repeat the same love experiences. This will cement your old beliefs and stunt your growth. What is your new definition of love? Or have you been carrying the same one since college? It doesn't matter if you're currently in a relationship or not. You can create a new definition at any time. As a matter of fact, you should. Because love is not a constant, and if you see it that way, your love will always flat-line. Love is its own living breathing thing that you must allow to constantly grow and evolve and take new shape as you grow and evolve and take new shape. Your partner should be creating their own new definitions as well. Both of you should be allowing this process to unfold and doing it together. That's what loving someone looks like. It's not just about hot sex and trying new restaurants. Your definitions don't have to match exactly. Most likely they won't. What's important is that you share the process with each other so you're doing life *with* and not *around* each other.

We've talked a lot about love. Now let's pull back and talk about life. Because there's more to life than love. This is true not only when you're single but especially when you're in a relationship. Many lose their life when they get into a relationship because their relationship becomes their life. If you don't have a life, you will eventually lose your relationship. Or never have a healthy one.

The Picket Fence Has Splinters

Barbara was a miserable fuck. Well, she didn't know it until she saw my book *I Used to Be a Miserable F*ck* at the airport. But she didn't buy it. The bold words on the cover caught her eye, and she saw that the book was written by a therapist. I think that's why she didn't buy it. She was also a therapist. Maybe she felt that if someone saw her picking it up, they would think her life wasn't perfect, that she was in no place to help others with theirs.

Barbara had a full practice, a solid marriage, beautiful kids, and a gorgeous craftsman home straight out of the pages of *Architectural Digest*. Literally. Her house was featured in the magazine. It's one of her "greatest" accomplishments. I saw the framed photo of the issue behind her desk while doing our online session. (Side note: It's strange to have a session with another therapist who is conducting it from her therapist chair. It's easy to get confused about who is actually the client.)

During our session, Barbara admitted that she was not happy and hadn't been for a long time. But she didn't realize it until she read my book, which she eventually ordered on Amazon so it would arrive discreetly, like a sex toy. She kept saying, "I should be happy. I have everything! A gorgeous home, a loving, caring, and supportive husband, and a thriving practice that took me over a decade to build. I don't know why I'm not happy."

Yes, she did have everything. Except for a life. Here's what she did every day. She got up at 7:00 a.m. Connected with her husband. Meditated. Had a quick breakfast. Then started taking sessions at 8:00 a.m. while her husband dropped the kids off at school. She worked from her home office, a cute little guesthouse with its own entrance. After a quick lunch break at noon, she returned to back-to-back sessions until 8:00 p.m.! Then she would have dinner with her family, catch up with her kids, make love to her husband (three nights a week), do some reading, go to bed, and start the process all over again the next day.

She had quality time with her family, but otherwise had basically created her own prison. As a therapist who had a full practice at one time, I know it can get very lonely. You can go on autopilot pretty quickly. She didn't have joy, engagement, or meaning in her life, the three things you need or you won't have a life. (I'll get into it in a bit.) Yes, she was a mom, and that was important to her, but her kids were in high school now. They had their own lives. Yes, she had a thriving therapy practice, but it was just a job now. She had lost the passion. She had burned out and was just going through the motions, addicted to the steady cash flow. And finally, her marriage was good in that there were no big problems or issues, but it was far from perfect. She and her husband made a great team, but the spark was gone. Dinners were pre-ordered. Sex was scheduled. Her marriage was on autopilot, just like the rest of her life.

We talked about what it would look like to inject her life with some joy, engagement, and meaning—what my life had been missing when I didn't really have one. Joy, engagement, and meaning gave me a life. I took off my therapist hat, put on my coaching hat, and helped her produce them.

Barbara discovered joy in doing therapy videos for social media. She admired what I was doing and secretly wanted to do the same but was afraid to. Once I challenged her definition of what a therapist looks like, she started using social media to create a dialogue. And she was really good at it. She had so much wisdom from her practice. She also started seeing a few of her clients on walks. This took her out of her house and into the world. She would have never done that while holding on to her old definitions of how a therapist should work.

Even while staying married, Barbara was being single on purpose. By threading these new patterns into her life, she found meaning and a sense of worth again. It wasn't that she found no meaning in her work. It was that she had been doing it in the same way for so long that she had lost her passion for it. Switching it up and approaching her work in new and exciting ways sparked a new love for her career.

The final piece was the most difficult for her: engagement.

Barbara had created a life that required little engagement with the outside world. Her home was her safe tree, and she rarely left it. After processing what engagement would look like for her, she started to step out. She made more of an effort to spend time with friends, which she'd stopped doing after having children. She started saying yes to social invites that she would have made an excuse to skip in the past.

It wasn't just about activities. I reminded Barbara that engagement is a mindset. Instead of watching the world, it was time for her to really live in it. To feel it with every fiber of her being, being fully present, and showing up as authentically herself. With positivity and a good attitude, hope and spontaneity. Engagement meant living outside of her own head and in her body, feeling things. Laughing. Crying. Loving. Being grateful.

She got it. And she started to thread engagement into her life. It didn't happen overnight, but gradually Barbara got a life.

A real one.

Not just something she could frame and hang over her desk.

How to Get a Life

We have been programmed to believe that happy is an island to swim to. And that, if we don't get there, we will never be happy. Our island may be the house, the love, the job, whatever. But happy does not live on an island. Happy is a state we can produce today. It's contingent on something else happening only if we make it that way. Happy is also not a constant. It comes and goes. There is an ebb and flow to happy. Some days it's easy to feel happy. Some days it's difficult. But happy starts with a choice, like everything else. Then creating a space that produces the feeling of happy. To do that, we must hang our lives on three things:

Meaning.

Joy.

Engagement.

Knowing this changed everything for me. Let me explain.

Meaning

I didn't have any meaning in my life before. Yes, I wanted things. But there was nothing in my life that really mattered to me besides my marriage. I spent hours in coffee shops hoping to sell a screenplay just to save my marriage. I wasn't making any money, and I'm sure that contributed to the expiration of the marriage. And what I was writing about wasn't meaningful. I was just writing up ideas I thought would sell. I didn't have meaning in other areas of my life either. I didn't have meaningful friends. Actually, I didn't have friends at all. I thought they were a waste of time. I didn't find meaning in spirituality, my relationship with my body, the universe, or my story. With no meaning in my life, nothing mattered. That left me two-dimensional and hollow. It's no wonder I was so miserable.

What exactly is meaning? It's not just about having a sense of purpose. Sure, a strong purpose can bring meaning into your life, a sense of worth and direction. But hanging your life on meaning doesn't just mean having purpose. You can have meaning in your life without a sense of purpose. Meaning just means whatever matters to you with where you're at in your life right now. Not yesterday. Not tomorrow. Right now, today. It's that simple. What matters to you and what doesn't? Are you investing in things that matter? I'm not talking about what matters to your friends or to the world. Things that matter to you!

This isn't just about what you do for work. What matters to you also includes relationships, friendships, and even what you want to eat for lunch, if that's meaningful to you today. No matter how big or small, if it's meaningful to you, you should invest in it. You can argue, "Well, drugs are meaningful to me right now." Okay, but are drugs truly meaningful, or are you using them as a way to cope because you don't have any meaning in your life? Meaning lines up with your truth and who you are. If you don't feed that, you will drift away from your truth and who you are. Everything from your taste in cars to how you want to make your dent in this world. If it's honest to you, it's meaningful. And if it's meaningful to you, it matters.

Today I still write. But not to sell. I write to help as many people as I can. It's meaningful to me. Even texting has become meaningful: I send out thousands of texts each day, hoping to give someone a new mindset or at least some kind of daily reminder. I have built friendships that are meaningful. I find meaning in my fitness. I use it to connect to my body. My motorcycle is meaningful. It brings me calm and a grin. I search for meaning in everything I do, and if I don't find it, I don't invest my time there. Any activity has to matter to me. Before, things didn't have to matter. I did things for approval, validation, or money. Today, if it's not meaningful to me, I'm not interested. I won't go back to living an unsubstantial life.

Most people do things that don't really matter to them. They invest in relationships that don't have much substance and do things because they feel like they *should*, not because they want to. Then they harbor anger and resentment, not only at others but at themselves. Carrying this low-grade anger starts to gray them out. They become moody and unhappy. Hanging your life on meaning allows you to be less angry and resentful. When you do things that truly matter to you, that line up with your truth and your story, you not only live closer to your potential but you become lighter, and lighter turns into happier.

Is what you're doing in your life truly meaningful to you? Do the relationships you're investing in truly matter?

Joy

The misconception about joy is that it just happens. That it falls into your lap. That you just close your eyes and take it in. That it's everywhere. Well, joy is in fact everywhere, but you have to look for it. There are skills involved.

I used to never feel much joy in my life because it never magically came. And even if it had, I wouldn't have felt it. I wasn't open to it. I didn't allow myself to feel joy unless something good happened. With this mindset, I rarely experienced joy, because it was contingent on something happening. That meant it was always in the distance. What I didn't understand was that joy is produced. And it's a practice.

You have to find joy in what you have today, no matter where you're at in your life or what you're going through. You can't put it off until you find your perfect love or get that amazing job or win the lottery. Most people believe that, and that's why they don't find joy. Finding joy is finding gold in quicksand. Finding good in bad. You have to train your brain to stop putting up impossible barriers to finding joy and discover it in what you have today.

This is where mindfulness and gratitude come into play. To become more aware and more grateful, start by training your brain to find joy in little things. Like the first stirrings of an idea. The first sip of your morning coffee. A breeze. A meaningful conversation. The feeling after a hard workout. None of these small joys are contingent on something big happening first. You can find them every single day by practicing the art of producing joy. I call it "seeking nectar," and a tattoo of a hummingbird on my left bicep reminds me to do just that.

Here is the nectar I seek to produce joy. I thread this practice into my daily life knowing I am training my brain and priming my state to experience more joy in my life.

- The joy of a quiet morning moment sipping fresh hot coffee. Not thinking about anything but just being present and taking in the moment, using all my senses. Waking up slowly.

- The joy of being creative. Writing, producing videos and podcasts, texting, whatever. Expressing myself in a way that's honest and makes me feel alive.

- The joy of social interactions. Making sure I connect with friends, being my authentic self while doing so. Expressing love and feeling loved.

- The joy of my daily sweat. Moving and connecting to my body, feeling the dopamine from pushing myself mentally as well as physically.

- The joy of a motorcycle ride. The adrenaline set pumping by an engine and two wheels. The feeling of the wind on my face. The music of the '80s.

- The joy of meals. Enjoying the food with intention. Trying different foods and restaurants.

- The joy of the human exchange in sessions with clients. Hearing and relating to stories. Connecting with and guiding another human. Allowing myself to be moved. Experiencing some kind of change after each session.

- The joy of learning about self-betterment and the human condition through audiobooks and videos.

- The joy of new daily revelations, big or small, through reflection. What comes when I notice and witness my thoughts and feelings instead of being hooked and drowning in them.

These daily practices produce joy for me. And I have them. They are mine. They are not contingent on something else happening. I have them now, and they bring me joy. I just have to seek them. Every day.

How are you producing joy in your life today?

Nothing Wrong Doesn't Mean There's Nothing Wrong

Trisha was sent to me by her husband. Like I've said, whenever someone is sent to me by someone else, it rarely works out. But Trisha admitted that she was depressed and didn't know why. She had a thriving company, a caring and loyal husband, good friends, and an impressive yoga practice. There was no trauma or darkness in her past. She didn't need to process anything like abuse. Her marriage wasn't falling apart. Her friendships weren't lopsided.

Because there was nothing wrong with her life, our sessions were like pulling teeth.

After a number of sessions, I realized that she didn't engage in her life. She had a solid structure and was extremely productive. But she didn't engage. She had no presence and made no eye contact. Trisha just kept herself aimed straight ahead and always moving forward. She wasn't living her life. Instead, she was watching it.

Exploring deeper, we discovered nothing specific that had happened that would have made her be this way. Her life had been years and years of safe routine that conditioned her to function on autopilot. So I coached her on practicing mindfulness. On getting still and engaging in the moment. Without judgment or intentions. Simply being. The practice was difficult for her. Like Chinese water torture in fact. For Trisha, there always needed to be a point to whatever she did. A reason. This requirement kept her moving on the outside, but on the inside she was dying. But she kept trying.

And then, the more she practiced engaging by being fully present and really showing herself by actively participating in moments and activities and with other people, the more people noticed things about her that they hadn't before. Little things. Like her quirky sense of humor. Trisha was actually funny. But more important, *she* noticed things about herself. Big things, small things, good things, bad things. Things that she hadn't before because she didn't engage. She had just watched her life. And she just watched because she was afraid. But the more she engaged in life, the more she discovered herself. And the more she discovered herself, the more she pulled herself out of her depression. Nothing wrong doesn't always mean there's nothing wrong.

Many of us forget that a rich colorful life doesn't just happen. We have to engage in it for color to appear, and it requires effort and intention. We can't just live on the sidelines and expect life to be bright. If we do, we will start to fade. Imagine life as a continuous flowing river. You are standing next to it. You can stand there and stare at your reflection. Or you can jump in and swim. If you just stand there, you are not living your life. You are watching it. You have to choose to engage, every single day.

Maybe you're saying, *But I do engage!* You get up, go to work, talk to people. Yes, you're getting there. But engagement isn't just about the activity. Engagement means showing up in your truest form every day. Showing up for everything. Whether you're in a boring work meeting or making love, engagement means being fully there in your truth. And that doesn't just happen naturally. It requires effort.

It doesn't really work if you engage in life only when things are good. You must engage even when things are bad. Especially when things are bad. Many people run or numb when life turbulence hits. To engage means to allow yourself to feel through the bad times, knowing it's not forever. If you're grieving, engage in it. If you're lonely or going through a breakup, engage in it. If you're going through a huge life transition, engage in it. Engaging even when things are bad doesn't mean allowing yourself to drown in it. It means experiencing all of life's seasons.

What does engagement look like? Calling friends and making an effort to hang out with them. Being vulnerable with your partner. Finally expressing how you feel. Even drawing boundaries is engagement. Engagement can mean jumping into the freezing ocean. Doing things out of your comfort zone. Switching shit up, like taking a different way home so you can see something new. Engagement can mean accepting, forgiving, apologizing, taking ownership.

Engagement can mean dancing even if you're embarrassed. It can simply mean getting out of your fucking house. Because not doing anything is not engagement.

Here's the thing: engagement means something different to everyone. You have to decide what engagement means to you.

My First
Mushroom Experience

We couldn't get into Joshua Tree. It was completely full. So we ended up setting up our two one-man tents, even though there were three of us, in a random desert junkyard on the outskirts. This was going to be my first time taking mushrooms, and it was already shady as fuck. I never did drugs growing up. I almost tried acid once, but the tab fell off my finger and I lost it in the grass. Anyway, when my friends found out I'd never done mushrooms, they convinced me to come with them to Joshua Tree to experience "real life magic." I was curious. So I went.

And here we were, sitting in a strange junkyard on lawn chairs in the middle of the night, staring out at a sea of ripped tires and broken trees. We had taken the shrooms a while before, but nothing was happening. I was frustrated. I kept yelling, "Nothing's happening! Nothing's happening! This is stupid!" And they kept yelling, "Calm the fuck down. Relax! Relax!" I hate when people tell me to relax. I was a high-strung kid, and when I was growing up everyone always told me to relax. It's a trigger for me. But I decided to shut up, sit there, and just wait. I had heard that on shrooms things morph into weird shapes and you see the world in ways you've never seen it before. But I felt nothing. The world stayed the same. Then I glanced over at Jeff. He was wearing a strange fishing hat. I said, "Why are you wearing a hat at night?" and just as I finished that sentence, I exploded in laughter. Which continued nonstop for the next two and a half hours. We all laughed uncontrollably. I laughed so hard my stomach started hurting. I wanted to stop but couldn't. I was angry but laughing at the same time. I literally crawled away holding my stomach, like someone shot me. I had to get away from them so I could stop laughing.

Eventually the laughter faded and we just sat there in the gutter of Joshua Tree, listening to music and watching the stars dance. It was probably the most present I've ever been in my life. Yes, it took drugs to get me out of my head, but I had a revelation that night: I realized the power of not living in time machines.

One of the most common things my clients struggle with is constantly being in their head, either dwelling on the past or obsessing about the future. I call this living in a time machine. It's something I struggle with as well. Here's how it works. Let me know if you can relate.

I have a thought about something that happened in the past. Maybe I play back a meaningful moment I had with an ex-girlfriend. That thought produces a feeling. That feeling makes me miss her. Now it's off to the races I go. Did I make a mistake by leaving? Should we be back together again? Should I call her? I wonder what she's doing. Am I with the wrong person now?

At this point, I am officially spinning. I have left the here and now and I am living in the past. Also, none of this is based on truth. It's based on a thought that produced a feeling. I can take it even further and reach out to my ex, but I'll quickly regret doing that when I remember all the reasons why the relationship ended. Or maybe I don't contact her. Maybe I just continue to ruminate on the thoughts and feelings. This keeps me in my head and not present in my current relationship. Distance and drift ripple into our intimacy. All because I allowed myself to be taken hostage by my thoughts.

Sound familiar? This is just one simple example. Imagine all the thoughts we have in a day and how many of them pull us out of the here and now and into a time machine. Thoughts not just about our past relationships but also about our work, friendships, drama in our family. Think about all the things you obsess about that haven't even happened yet. What if you don't make the sale? Get the raise? Pass the test? What if you never find "the one"? Thoughts like these produce feelings of anxiety. Suddenly, we are drowning in what-ifs instead of living in *what is*. We have left our lives because our heads have taken us hostage.

It's time machines that cripple us the most when we are single. We live in them. More than when we are in a relationship, we dwell on our past and obsess about our future. Because when we love someone, we don't think about ourselves. We think about our partner or about the relationship. We think about what our partner wants and how we can give them that. How we can be better. For someone else. We think about our relationship and how we can make it stronger. We think about where to go for dinner, what movies to watch, who we'll invite over for game night.

But when we're single, we're left alone with ourselves. This can be an uncomfortable place we don't like sitting in, one we're not used to. So we search for someone else so we can be part of something else. We grab the side of the pool so we don't have to swim. So we don't have to face ourselves. If we can't find someone to hold on to, we default to what was and what will be. Like a flipped magnet, we can't stay present in the here and now because that's where all our insecurities live. So we live in time machines without realizing that dwelling on the past and the future creates nothing but anxiety.

How to Stop Living in a Time Machine

STEP 1

Notice how often you play back the past or imagine the future. Be aware of how you feel in your body when you do. What are the feelings produced by playing this movie? And where do those feelings lead you? Do you feel empowered? Or discouraged and hopeless? Do you play back all the what-ifs and wonder what life would have been like if things had happened differently? Or what could happen but hasn't yet and what if it never does? How does it make you feel knowing that you can't change the past or know the future? Most likely, not good. Now, do you blame and judge others or yourself for this being the way things are? Do you internalize it? Do you bash yourself for making the choices you did in the past? Do you feel less than because you don't have a clear future?

If so, you have lost yourself. You are also now officially traveling at light speed. You need to get back before you starting engaging in unhealthy behaviors to cope. Before you turn to your vices to feel better. Before you punish yourself. Before you allow the past or the future, or, more accurately, your judgment of yourself, to affect your present. Where truth actually lives.

Follow this tread. A thought leads to a feeling, which leads to internalization, which leads to certain behaviors. See where that first thought leads you? Do you like where it leads you? Is it healthy and positive? Or is it unhealthy, producing anxiety and panic?

STEP 2

Break the pattern. Don't allow your thoughts to hook you. See them. Notice them. But even as you keep an eye on them, create distance so they cannot take you hostage. Your thoughts are not you. They are just thoughts, produced by judgment and distortion. That's why you must create distance from them. Imagine your thoughts in a snow globe. Watch them there. Don't own them. Allow yourself to feel your feelings, but know that they are just that—feelings. Not facts or truth. Feelings will flow through you. And then they will pass.

STEP 3

Create new thoughts and feelings. Think about things that make you feel hopeful. That make the world wide instead of narrow and dark. Think about what you've learned from the past instead of the ways in which you want to change it. Add new thoughts to your mental conveyer belt. Choose what you want to think about. Keep your thoughts positive and your feelings will be positive. Instead of thoughts that lead to anxiety and panic, think thoughts that produce feelings of gratitude and joy. Play a different movie.

STEP 4

Do steps 1 through 3 and then repeat. Forever.

Step 4 is the most important piece. People think that, if they practice these steps for a weekend, they can destroy their time machine. Think about what you're trying to do here. You're trying to undo years and years of wiring and deeply ingrained thinking patterns. So it's going to take time to rewire yourself. It's going to take a daily practice. Just as it does to change a body. Meditation can help tremendously. Meditation will create that distance you need. It will lay down a speed bump so you don't jump from thought to feeling to an overly quick reaction. Breathe. Notice. Don't judge. Create distance. Allow.

After spending a day doing this practice, ask yourself: How did that feel? Did you feel different about your day because of it? If so, how? Were you able to be more present? Did you have less anxiety?

Now try to thread together more days like this one.

Rip Up Your Blueprints

Whether you are aware of it or not, the blue-prints stamped in our heads are where we pull from. Our lives follow our tracings of these blueprints. For example, say your definition or blueprint of a happy life is a white picket fence, two kids, and matching BMWs. But you're in your late thirties and unmarried, you don't have kids, and you drive a Honda. Most likely, you are not happy, because your life doesn't match the blueprint in your head. The greater the contrast between your blueprint and your actual life, the more anxious and unhappy you are. So now you have two choices.

Option one is to go all out trying to match that blueprint—find a man, make babies, buy a house. This option will probably require compromising on who you choose to love. You'll negotiate about your needs and what you deserve because your clock is ticking. This relationship is likely to become unhealthy and toxic, but you have kids with him and that's what counts, because kids are part of your blueprint. On a deeper level, you may be having kids to distract yourself from the problems in your marriage. Which is shitty: you're raising your kids by yourself because the drift has caused both you and your partner to check out emotionally and physically. Eventually you'll have had enough and you'll get a divorce. You'll feel like a complete failure. Now you're in your late forties and have to start life all over.

Option two is to toss your blueprint.

Our blueprints are created by our definitions. Our definition of happy, love, healthy, success, everything. Many of us live with definitions that were given to us by parents, friends, society, advertising, and old versions of ourselves that are not honest to us anymore. By following these definitions, we start to live dishonest lives. Or we live someone else's life. Ultimately, either response causes disconnection and unhappiness.

Here are some common blueprints we try to trace:

> Get married and have kids before we turn thirty
>
> Get a college degree so we can land a six-figure job with great benefits
>
> Buy a house (which means we've made it)
>
> Have our own business (because working for someone else means we're not successful)

Here are some common definitions we carry:

> Divorce means we've failed and/or we're defective.
>
> Not having kids means something's wrong with us.

If we're single, something's wrong with us.

Without a college education, we will never be successful.

Love means giving everything.

Vulnerability is a weakness.

Here's the blueprint I used to try to trace when I was a miserable fuck. It was my definition of success.

A beautiful wife

A house in the Hollywood Hills

A three-picture deal as a screenwriter, with an office on a studio lot

The Porsche–Range Rover combo in the driveway

This blueprint was the vision I had tacked to the front of my mind. It was what I compared my life to daily. Everything revolved around acquiring these things. And since I didn't have them, I didn't allow myself to be happy. There's nothing wrong with wanting a house in the Hills, a studio deal as a screenwriter, and nice cars. But this blueprint was very two-dimensional, spelling out only things to pursue. Nowhere did this blueprint address the need to develop a sense of self. This blueprint didn't help me come to know who I was. All I knew was that I wanted to be "successful." Though of course my definition of success was also two-dimensional.

Here's my blueprint today.

I still want a house in the Hills. I still want nice cars and a few motorcycles. But those are just things produced by living a meaningful life. By running toward your true north. I also want to help people. I want to create a dialogue. I want to write books. I want to be a good person. I don't just want to have things. I want to do things that are meaningful. I want to like myself. I want to live an honest life and feel like I'm making a dent in this world. I want to be a student of life and continue to learn. I want to love and to grow as a spiritual being. I want to be a dad.

With this blueprint, I'm not just chasing things. Instead, I'm looking inward with a desire to grow and be better so I can share my story and help others. The things detailed in this blueprint are just by-products of that. This blueprint is about growth and new revelations. Not about houses and cars and a hot wife. Tracing this blueprint is more likely to put me in an attracting state because I'm living inside out instead of outside in. And since our gifts live in who we are, when we actively work more on who we are instead of just going after what we want, the chances of great things happening grow exponentially. We start attracting instead of just chasing. One state is power-filled. The other makes us powerless.

TIME TO MAKE SHIT HAPPEN

Ask yourself if your blueprint is honest to you or if you're tracing something that's old or that belongs to someone else.

Create new definitions. It's time to redefine everything, in ways that are honest to you today. With where you're at and with everything you've learned about life and love and yourself up until now.

What does love look like?

What does success look like?

What does dating look like?

What does fitness look like?

What does self-care look like?

What does being spiritual look like?

What does singlehood look like?

Reworth Yourself

f I had to pick one single gift I received from my single-hood journey that not only changed my behavior and energy—and ultimately my life—but also repositioned me and helped me be happier and feel more whole and human, it was finally believing that I have worth. Not in an egotistical way. Not in an "I'm better than anyone else" way, but in an "I'm not perfect but I like myself enough to invest in me" way. I finally believe I bring value to relationships and have something to offer the world. Before I started doing everything I recommend in this book to connect and build a relationship with myself, I didn't believe I had any value. My worth came from what I accomplished, and my lack of worth from what I didn't accomplish. It came from who chose to love me. This belief left me feeling powerless and, of course, feeling less worthy.

Most of my clients are in this place when they first come to see me. They don't believe they have value. That's why they are so desperately wanting to be with someone—to prove they have worth. That's why they compromise and tolerate toxic relationships. That's why they stay in shitty jobs that don't allow them to thrive. That's why their friendships are lopsided and their marriages are broken and lukewarm at best. That's why they don't truly engage in life. Instead, they live in fear and allow the world and others to paint their life with brushes and colors that are not honest to them. The result is a blurry abstract painting of their life that they are not proud of. Their life has become cheap art they are embarrassed to hang instead of a work of art they will leave behind for others to appreciate and enjoy.

Everything ends and begins with what you believe about yourself. What you believe will determine where you will go. And who you will become.

But here's the thing. Believing you have value isn't just an announcement or a decision. It may start there. But truly believing you have value requires years of rebuilding your relationship with yourself. You are rewiring deeply ingrained thinking and beliefs that may have been formed by trauma, abusive relationships, and a scarred childhood. Before you could drive, these imprints were formed by circumstances you had no control over and by people who pulled from reactions tied to their own worth, or lack thereof. We all have been in situations or relationships that made us question our worth. We all have been tested, treated unfairly, bullied, lied to, cheated on, ghosted, and gaslighted. Add to that failed marriages, businesses that go belly up, friendships that end abruptly, family members who disown us—the things that happen to everyone. We tie all of that to our worth, letting the external events of our lives determine our internal beliefs about ourselves.

You may be one of the many who have not escaped this dynamic, but you can heal. You can rebuild. You can get to a place where you start to believe you are worth something. And you have to. Because if you don't, you will never give yourself new experiences that change your old beliefs. You will never build healthy spaces for yourself that promote growth. You will never make better choices because you'll keep on saying no when you need to say yes. Instead, you will default to the same and allow *what was* to block who you could be.

When you believe you are worth something, the universe moves.

So instead of allowing your past to drown you and staying stuck in negative thought patterns that dilute your being, strip your soul, and smash your dreams, it's time to reworth yourself and generate energy that punctures space and grabs stars.

So how do you do this? How do you start to believe you are worth more?

Start here: Worth is not something you believe. **Worth is something you build.** Read that sentence again. Most people think they can white-knuckle their way to worth. But you can't. It's a process. More accurately, a space.

You can fantasize and dream about who you want to be and how you want to feel, but until you actually give yourself a new experience, your beliefs about yourself will most likely not change. There's nothing more convincing, though, than a new experience.

New experiences → Shifts in beliefs → New definitions → More new experiences

What new experience do you have to give yourself so that your beliefs about yourself will shift and change as you create new definitions? Once you have new definitions, you will create new experiences based on those definitions, which will give you new experiences that will shift more beliefs. This is the pattern that will start to rewire you.

> Do you need to experience the feeling of singlehood for a while so that you know you can be single?
>
> Do you need to give yourself a healthy love experience so that you know what that feels like?
>
> Do you need to find a workout that you truly enjoy so you can give yourself the experience of actually liking movement?
>
> Do you need to give yourself the experience of doing work you're passionate about so that you won't have to dread work anymore?
>
> What experiences do you need to give yourself?

This process may seem overwhelming. So know that it's a marathon, not a 100-meter dash. And it's a marathon that never ends. It's a mindset and a way of living. You will continue to seek out new experiences that shift your beliefs and build your worth. Because life will keep coming at you. Things will happen that cut you down at the knees. Someone will break your heart. Again. You will always be tested and questioned. But if you stop pedaling the bike (giving yourself new experiences), you will stop moving (growing and building worth).

Start with one new experience. It doesn't have to be life-changing. It can be small. Like holding a conversation without judgment. Like raising your hand in the boardroom and speaking your truth. Like pushing yourself in a new workout more than you ever pushed yourself before. Like making a decision from passion instead of from logic.

Do everything you can to give yourself that experience before moving on to more and more new experiences. Know that by giving yourself new experiences, you are building your worth.

Live at a Higher Frequency

'm sure you've heard of living at a higher frequency before, but like most people, you probably haven't made a conscious effort to raise the frequency you live at and stay there. Higher frequencies include love, gratitude, optimism, joy, acceptance, courage, vulnerability—basically any state that pulls you out of panic and negativity. Any state that fills you with hope and optimism. Any state that expands you instead of constricts you. This is not a mental thing. It's a mind–body–energy thing. The higher the frequency you live on, the lighter you feel physically, emotionally, and mentally. But the challenge isn't to get there. We can all feel love and optimism at times. What's difficult is to stay there.

So what does living at a higher frequency have to do with your worth?

I spent most of my twenties and thirties in a lower frequency. Mostly the low-frequency states of worry and dread. Worried about tomorrow. Dreading today. Day in and day out. Worry and dread. Dread and worry. It was nearly impossible to believe I had any value because this state blocked me from giving myself new experiences that would shift my beliefs about myself and what was possible and inject some hope into my life. Instead, the state of worry and dread kept me stuck and swimming in my own shit.

It wasn't until many relationships expired and I found myself feeling neither happy nor alive that I finally decided to draw a hard line. I realized that my lower frequency—my negative state—was affecting not just me but others as well. I was taking hostages. It was time to change. So I started to pay attention to when my faulty thinking, faulty attitude, or faulty perspective dropped me into a lower frequency, and I started doing everything I could to pull myself out of it.

There was no manual. Maybe like you, I was armed only with inspirational YouTube videos and memes about gratitude on my social media feed. Yes, I had a therapy degree, but that didn't make anything easier. Because here's the thing: you can't just force yourself to go to a higher frequency. It doesn't happen just because you've made a decision and don't want to live at a low frequency anymore.

I was sick of making excuses. So I went cold turkey. I made a promise to myself that I would be aware of when I dropped into a lower frequency and do everything I could to raise myself out of it.

Here's what I did.

STEP 1

When I felt myself dipping into a lower frequency, I would do two things:

1. I created distance from my thoughts that were making me feel this way. I would do this through meditation, a walk, or a motorcycle ride. Maybe by having coffee with a friend. Sometimes with an ice bath. I did whatever would help me that day to release my hold on the thoughts that were about to drown me.

2. Using my body was often the fastest way to kick up my frequency. I would drop into my body by doing something physical to make my body feel light again. Like working out or going for a run.

Many of us can't just leave work and go do something active. But we can all go for a quick walk. Even if it's for five minutes. I'd listen to something when I went for a walk—a podcast or a song, and sometimes an audio recording I'd made to remind myself that I was an addict, dropping into negativity was my drug, and I was about to fucking use, so stop. For me, the consequence of dropping into this lower frequency was losing the life I wanted. I had to create that kind of urgency for myself. I had to tell myself that my life was at stake, because the truth is, it was.

STEP 2

I explored and questioned where this pattern of pessimism came from. I realized that it started at an early age. The worry came from my dad, who also struggled with being in this lower-frequency state. Yes, he was fun and gregarious at times. But mostly he put his adult worries about money and bills and work and being in debt onto his sons. One reason he did this may have been cultural: Koreans see the family as a unit. My brother and I were deeply affected. Being burdened by Dad's worries made my brother grow up very fast. He became an adult at thirteen, the responsible one. I tried to escape the stress by going outside to play with friends. But I had to come home sometime, and when I did, I felt it. I absorbed it.

Once you discover the origin of your tendency to fall into a low-frequency state, you can create distance and compassion. If you don't figure it out, you'll get angry at yourself for being in this state. You'll internalize that anger and bash yourself with it—the complete opposite of building self-worth. Internalized anger at yourself destroys self-worth.

This piece is just as important as the hard line you drew. There is power and healing in understanding what has made you the way you are. It neutralizes and builds a bridge that makes your change to living at higher frequencies more of an evolution than a matter of willpower.

It's Time to Believe Again

Why is it time to believe again? Because you did at one point. We all did. Before the drama. The chaos. The patterns. The partners. The fall. Before the abandonment, the ghosting, the checking-out. Before the unexpected events. Before the termination, the false beliefs, the internal death. Before the marriage, the babies, the breakup, and the corner office.

When you believed before, the world was big. The day was wide. Anything was possible. Not like today, when the day feels narrow and stifling. It's time. To believe. In love. In sweat. In building something. In starting over. Because over doesn't mean again. Over means new. But you can't get to new until you believe. Again.

What you believe will determine whether you truly live or just exist. It's time to believe, because everything starts or ends there.

Final Thoughts:
Every. Single. Day.

In conclusion, I just want to share a reminder with you. A mantra. It's on a magnet on my fridge (it's a big magnet). I wrote it when I was single. It's helped me through all my singlehood journeys and continues to help me today. I hope it helps you as well.

Every. Single. Day.

Know that you are valuable. Start your day like it's your last. Seek nectar. Stretch your bright spots. Shatter your veneer. Practice transparency. Love hard. Dream big. Sweat daily. Resist nothing. Embrace your story. It's the only one you've got. Don't feed negativity. Don't engage with negative people. Don't live in the past. Fuck your identity. Crush your false beliefs. Prove yourself wrong. Run toward your fears instead of away. Throw your stone as hard as you can, knowing that it will send ripples. Be a prism, not a rock. Drink water. Ask questions. Turn your dial to give. Don't gossip. Don't seek approval or validation. Get out of your head. It's the most dangerous place. Don't react. Respond. Eat well, not more. Do things alone. Understand before you speak. Burn your boats. Lean forward. Forgive. Know somebody. And go to bed with fucking gratitude.

Single On Purpose Mixtape

U sually we make mixtapes for our partner. Why can't we make one for ourselves? Below are a few songs I listened to on many singlehood journeys. Walking the streets of Koreatown alone. Riding my motorcycle, hugging canyons. Pushing through burpees at the gym. I hope you make yourself your own mixtape. While you're going on long night walks, working out, eating pancakes at a diner at midnight, dancing in your kitchen while learning to cook, taking solo road trips, doing shrooms—wherever your singlehood journey takes you.

"This Must Be the Place"—Talking Heads

It doesn't matter what mood I'm in, this song always cheers me up. It just makes me happy. Maybe because the '80s were my wonder years. I like to go there often. "Feet on the ground. Head in the sky. It's okay, I know nothing's wrong." There's an innocence to this song, a simplicity. My favorite line is "I see light in your eyes." It reminds me what to look for in people.

"Anything Anything"—Dramarama

This is my "rocking out in my underwear in my bedroom" song. Nothing makes me feel more like a sixteen-year-old again, in a good way. That age before I knew what consequences were. When love was just a magical feeling you would die for. Before the meetings. Before therapy. Before my rebirth. I like listening to this song while driving very fast on two or four wheels, but if it's four, there can't be a roof.

"California Stars"—Wilco

This was the theme song for the dirt bike trip I took from Sequoia to Yosemite. Twelve dudes, eighty miles a day, campfires, woods, rocks, dirt, dust, adrenaline, and stars. It reminds me to seek adventure, appreciate nature, and practice mindfulness.

"Float On"—Modest Mouse

A reminder that we'll "all float on okay." This waters me with a sense of calm. Allows me to let go of the rock and let the river of life take me. On my back. Eyes soaking in the sun. A grin on my face. This too will pass. The sky will not fall. Everything will be okay.

"Seven Wonders"—Fleetwood Mac

This song makes me cry. It's magical as fuck and makes me believe in something bigger. Past lives. Stars. The universe. There is more than just what I can see or what I think I know. I listen to it often on longer trips on my Harley as

I connect the dots of my story. As I look at life through a larger lens. I haven't seen any of the seven wonders. I will one day.

"Golden Light"—STRFKR

The backbeat of this song is what moved me. I never even listened to the words. Structure. Building. Sweating. Eating better. Patience. Trust. Keeping going. The power of momentum. And the daily grind of building a better you. Sometimes you don't need words to move you.

"Overkill"—Men at Work

Ktown. Struggling with loneliness. In the middle of my dark tunnel. Insomnia. But still standing. Knowing it will be all right. Thinking about everything I've been through and how far I've come. Telling the pain to come back another day.

"Running to Stand Still"—U2

Like I did on the beach that day.

"The Background"—Third Eye Blind

The sound that we carry with us when the relationship is gone. Like a note we know we must burn one day. Reminds me of high school and young love. But not in a bad way.

"Miss You"—Ringside

Because it's okay to miss someone, even if you know there's nothing you can do to keep from running away.

"You Make My Dreams"—Hall & Oates

I can't not do the Carlton dance whenever I hear this song. It made me smile on the tough days, the days I didn't want to feel heavy.

"Disconnected"—Face to Face

One of my faves from high school. It made not knowing what you want okay. And it still did in my thirties as I blasted this tune in my two-seater convertible through the canyons, sporting my nonprofit uniform with a *DSM-IV* in my truck and wondering who I would be in five years.

"Get Hurt"—The Gaslight Anthem

This song helped me sit in the pain. Not suffering. Just feeling. Sitting in the hurt. Until it turned into a story. One I could accept and eventually let go. I blasted this song while flying my arm out the window on the Pacific Coast Highway, feeling the California sun on my face and wondering, "Maybe you needed a change. Maybe I was in the way."

"There Is a Light That Never Goes Out"—The Smiths

Another high school song I dusted off and played often. Reminded me of controlled recklessness. The spirit of us living forever. Tragedy not being that bad. "Take me anywhere. I don't care. I don't care. I don't care."

"Holiday in Spain"—Counting Crows

My fantasy song. I imagined getting on a plane and leaving the residue of what had happened. Leaving all my worries behind. Flying away to somewhere new. To a beautiful girl waiting for me in Mexico. To a place where no one knew me. Where I could rediscover myself. I played this song often as I rode my motorcycle around LA and let this fantasy fly.

"Sweetest Kill"—Broken Social Science

This song reminded me of the predator-and-prey dynamic. Wondering, as I was going through my rebirth and self-evaluation, following strings in my story, if I was a predator. The instinctual draw, reviewed. How many of the women I loved were prey? Realizing the power of primal attraction. How much of our dysfunction was wiring? Did she even know?

"Never Tear Us Apart" (live)—The Horrible Crows

This song reminded me of how I used to believe in forever. The lightning in the bottle. The knowing. The locking eyes from across the room. The "I was standing here and you were there." A collision that creates secondary change and deep imprints that we compare all our other love experiences to. The early love experience that eventually turns love into a hot stove. This song reminded me of what I had thought was healthy love.

"Suffer Well"—Depeche Mode

When I played this song, I felt like suffering wasn't a bad thing. Because pain can be soil. And that's what makes you hang on. What makes you believe. I played this song often on long night walks. It made the hurt okay. Made me believe it was all a part of life. The process. My evolution. It made me suffer well.

"Ain't Nobody"—Chaka Khan

I used to break-dance to this song in the '80s. So listening to it thirty years later connected me back to my younger self. I was learning to dance again, but this time on a pull-up bar. The building, the growing, the earning of sweat. The reminder that nobody will ever love you better than yourself. A reminder of doing head spins and chasing flow states when life was simple and love was just an idea.

Resources

You can find the full playlist on my Instagram. Just click my bio link: @theangrytherapist.

I also text people daily. You can wake up to a reminder, a new perspective, or a fresh mindset to help you with your day. At the end of each week, I'll text you a private link to a Google Doc on a new topic that will take you deeper into that week's topic. Get your daily texts at www.theangrytherapist .com.

See you in your phone.

Acknowledgments

Thanks to Laura Yorke (my literary agent) for being a real person not just an agent. For believing in me and treating me like family. For guiding me, teaching me the ropes, and making me spaghetti in New York. Thank you for helping me fall in love with writing again.

Thanks to Hilary Swanson (my editor) for taking a chance on me. Again. For loving books and fighting for voices. For showing up to my signings. For being the easiest editor on earth to work with. Without you, my books would be unreadable. You make me a better writer. Thank you for your taste, your touch, and your trust.

Thanks to everyone on the HarperOne dream team for making this possible. For your support and belief in me. For your permission to ride the edge and speak my truth. Thanks to Aidan Mahony, for your eyes and fresh perspective.

Thanks to Vanessa (my girlfriend), for being such a supportive and loving partner. For reading my horrible drafts. For believing in me. For sharing your singlehood journey with me and hearing mine as well. Without judgment. For choosing to love me every day, even when it's hard. For being you. And of course, for making us a baby. I hope she reads this book one day and it helps her connect to herself. Thank you for holding my yesterday, dancing with my today, and helping us build our tomorrow.